The Memorandum

Václav Havel

The Memorandum

Translated from the Czech
by Vera Blackwell

Introduction by
Tom Stoppard

Grove Weidenfeld
New York

Published by Grove Weidenfeld
A division of Wheatland Corporation
841 Broadway
New York, NY 10003-4793

LIBRARY OF CONGRESS CATALOGING-IN-PUBLICATION DATA
Havel, Václav.
    The memorandum.
    Translation of Vyrozumeni.
    I.   Title.
PG5039.18.A9V913   1980   891.8'625   79-28731
ISBN 0-8021-3229-4

Manufactured in the United States of America

Printed on acid-free paper

First Evergreen Edition 1980

10   9   8   7   6   5   4   3

INTRODUCTION

Václav Havel's career as a playwright has been brief in his own country. It began with *The Garden Party* in 1963, and was suspended in 1968 by the Husak regime which took power in the wake of the Soviet invasion a few months after Havel's third play, *The Increased Difficulty of Concentration,* had opened in Prague. *The Memorandum* is the play that came between those two, in 1965.

Despite the ban on performances of his work in Czechoslovakia, Havel has continued to write, and latterly has produced a doppelganger, a playwright and persona-non-grata named Ferdinand Vanek whose adventures are sardonically recalled, so far, in three short plays, *Audience, Private View,* and *Protest.* Even so, *The Memorandum* possibly remains his most widely performed play, and the one which best shows off the hallmarks of his gift: the fascination with language; the invention of an absurd society raised only a notch or two above the normal world of state bureaucracy; the absurdities pushed to absurdity compounded by absurdity and yet saved from mere nonsense by their internal logic; and, not least, the playfulness with which it is done, the almost gentle refusal to indulge a sense of grievance, the utter lack of righteousness or petulance or bile—the same quality, in fact, which was to distinguish the Vanek plays ten years later, by which time Havel might have been forgiven for writing with bitterness.

For let it be said that while this edition of *The Memorandum* was being prepared for the press (April 1980), its author was entering the sixth month of a four-and-a-half-year prison sentence meted out for crimes which have no counterpart in a free society.

Havel's first spell in prison was in 1977. He had been arrested in January soon after the appearance of Charter 77, a document calling upon the Czech government to abide by its own laws. Havel, as one of three designated spokesmen for the Charter and the best known, was kept in prison for four months and ultimately given a suspended sentence of fourteen months. Despite his extreme vulnerability, he associated himself the following year with the Committee for the Defence of the Unjustly Persecuted (VONS in the Czech acronym). Eleven members of VONS were arrested in March 1979 and six of these, including Havel, were brought to trial in October, when the very existence of VONS was defined as an act of subversion. A proper account of those proceedings and a proper recognition of the other defendants would be in order, but to a prospective reader of *The Memorandum* the most pertinent echo from that trial is that of the words spoken by Havel to his judges before he was sentenced. Needless to say, no official record exists and the quotation does not claim to be verbatim, but nevertheless this is what the author of this play had to say:

"The system is based on an a priori assumption that the state can do no wrong. The decision of a court is regarded as being infallible in principle. I want to stress that this assumption of infallibility is very dangerous. Anyone who questions it is automatically defined as an enemy and everything he does is qualified as hostile. If the institutions of the state can never be in error, then anybody criticizing their actions is logically engaging in slander, vilification, and so on. And why should somebody vilify? Naturally, out of hostility. And if out of hostility, then, naturally, in collusion with a foreign, hostile and anti-socialist power. The indictment does not mention what should be the crucial issue—the contents of the VONS statements. The prosecution cannot allow any consideration of what VONS actually said, because to allow that would be tantamount to conceding the possibility of the state's fallibility....If you write that student X copied a piece by Václav Havel and gave it to his fellow students to read, it does not sound nearly so serious as it does when you write that "Student X duplicated and distributed in an illegal manner an anti-socialist pamphlet by a right-wing exponent." There are certain words which recur continually in the indictment and which one would describe as loaded, words like subversion, lies, malice, illegal organizations, anti-communist centers, vilification, hatred, and so on. However, when one looks closely at these words, one finds that there is nothing behind them."

If, as nowadays, one might easily suppose the proper study of Literary Man is the intersection of a writer's work and his experience, what a gift that statement seems to offer: here is a play about words, infallibility, logic and the system.

Yet to make too much of that would be to distract attention from the inventiveness of *The Memorandum*. We are introduced to a new official language, Ptydepe, designed to banish the confusions of natural, unscientific language, and based on maximizing the difference between words so that no word can conceivably be mistaken for another, the length of a word being proportional to the frequency of use (the word for wombat has 319 letters). Alas, Ptydepe begins to assume some of the characteristics of a natural language, emotional overtones, ambiguities, and so on, and is therefore replaced by a new language, Chorukor, whose principle is to maximize the resemblance between words, so that Monday becomes "Ilopagar," Tuesday "Ilopager," etc., and the worst that can happen is that the right things will occur on the wrong day of the week.

In the lifelike encounters of the Vanek plays, experience does indeed provide a template for art, but here one relishes the joyous freedom of Havel's imagination. In 1965 joy and freedom seemed possible.

—TOM STOPPARD

LIST OF CHARACTERS

JOSEF GROSS	*Managing Director*
JAN BALLAS	*Deputy Director*
OTTO STROLL	*Head of the Translation Center*
ALEX SAVANT	*Ptydepist*
HELENA	*Chairman*
MARIA	*Secretary at the Translation Center*
HANA	*Secretary to the Managing Director*
MARK LEAR	*Teacher of Ptydepe*
FERDINAND PILLAR	
GEORGE	*Staff Watcher*
PETER THUMB	*A clerk*
MR. COLUMN	
THREE CLERKS	

The action takes place in three office rooms within one large organization. Each office differs from the other in its particulars (placing of furniture, office equipment, etc.), but they all exude the same atmosphere and thus resemble each other. In each, there are two exits: a back door (B.D.) and a side door (S.D.).

SCENE 1

The Director's office. Large office desk, small typist's desk, a fire extinguisher on the wall, a coat rack in the background. The stage is empty. Then GROSS *enters by B.D., takes off his coat, hangs it on the rack, sits at his desk and begins to go through his morning mail. He skims each letter, then puts it either into waste-paper basket or into out tray. One letter suddenly arrests his attention. He glares at it and then starts to read it aloud.*

GROSS *(reads)*: Ra ko hutu d dekotu ely trebomu emusohe,
vdegar yd, stro reny er gryk kendy, alyv zvyde dezu,
kvyndal fer tekynu sely. Degto yl tre entvester kyleg
gh : orka epyl y bodur depty-depe emete. Grojto
af xedob yd, kyzem ner osonfterte ylem kho dent de
det detrym gynfer bro enomuz fechtal agni laj kys
defyj rokuroch bazuk suhelen. Gakvom ch ch lopve
rekto elkvestrete. Dyhap zuj bak dygalex ibem
nyderix tovah gyp. Ykte juh geboj. Fyx dep butrop
gh—
*(*GROSS *does not notice that meanwhile* BALLAS *and* PILLAR *have quietly entered by S.D.* BALLAS *coughs discreetly.)*
GROSS: Are you here?
BALLAS: Yes, we are.
GROSS: I didn't hear you come in.
BALLAS: We entered quietly.
GROSS: Have you been here long?
BALLAS: Not long.
GROSS: What is it?

3

BALLAS: We've come to ask your advice, Mr. Gross.

GROSS: Go on.

BALLAS: Where should Mr. Pillar record the incoming mail?

GROSS: Couldn't be more obvious, Mr. Ballas. In the incoming-mail book.

BALLAS: It's full, isn't it, Mr. P.?
(PILLAR nods.)

GROSS: So soon?

BALLAS: I'm afraid so.

GROSS: Good gracious! Well, he'll have to get a new one.

BALLAS: We've no funds to get a new one, have we, Mr. P.?
(PILLAR shakes his head.)

GROSS: What do you mean no funds? As far as I recall a purchase of two incoming-mail books was budgeted for this quarter.

BALLAS: It was. But in accordance with the new economy drive all budgeted expenditures were cut by half, with the result that we were able to purchase only one incoming-mail book which is, as I've just mentioned, full. Isn't it, Mr. P.?
(PILLAR nods.)

GROSS *(hands PILLAR some money)*: Here. Buy yourself a new one.
(PILLAR pockets the money. Both bow respectfully.)

BALLAS: We thank you, Mr. Gross. Thank you very much.
(They leave by S.D. GROSS picks up his letter and examines it with curiosity. HANA enters by B.D., wearing a coat and carrying a vast shopping bag.)

HANA: Good morning.

GROSS *(without looking up)*: Good morning.
(HANA hangs her coat on coat rack, sits down at typist's desk, takes a mirror and a comb out of her bag, props mirror against typewriter and begins to comb her hair. Combing her hair will be

4

her main occupation throughout the play. She will
interrupt it only when absolutely necessary. GROSS
watches her stealthily for a moment, then turns to
her.)

GROSS: Hana—

HANA: Yes, Mr. Gross?

GROSS *(shows her the letter)*: Any idea what this is?

HANA *(skims the letter)*: This is a very important office
    memorandum, Mr. Gross.

GROSS: It looks like a hodgepodge of entirely haphazard
    groups of letters.

HANA: Perhaps, at first glance. But in fact there's
    method in it. It's written in Ptydepe, you see.

GROSS: In what?

HANA: In Ptydepe.

GROSS: In Ptydepe? What is it?

HANA: A new office language which is being introduced
    into our organization. May I go and get the milk?

GROSS: There's a new language being introduced into
    our organization? I don't remember having been
    informed.

HANA: They must have forgotten to tell you. May I
    go and get the milk;

GROSS: Who thought it up?

HANA: It seems to be a full-scale campaign. Elsie said
    it's being introduced into their department, too.

GROSS: Does my deputy realize what's going on?

HANA: Mr. Ballas? Of course he does. May I go and
    get the milk?

GROSS: Run along.
    (HANA takes empty bottle from her shopping bag
    and hurries out by B.D. GROSS paces thought-
    fully up and down. Again does not notice when
    BALLAS and PILLAR enter by S.D. BALLAS
    coughs.)

GROSS: Are you here again?

BALLAS: We've come to tell you that we've just pur-
    chased a brand new incoming-mail book. It's lying
    on Mr. Pillar's desk. Isn't it, Mr. P.?

5

(PILLAR nods.)

GROSS: Good.

BALLAS: But the Department of Authentication refuses to authenticate it.

GROSS: Why?

BALLAS: The new book hasn't been registered by the Purchasing Department on account of its not having been purchased with the department's funds. So, legally, it doesn't exist, does it, Mr. P.?
(PILLAR shakes his head.)

GROSS: Say I ask them to authenticate it on my personal responsibility. My position's solid now, I think I can go so far.

BALLAS: Excellent! Would you mind giving it to us in writing? It'll simplify things a great deal.

GROSS: I would. I don't mind taking risks, but I'm not a gambler. A verbal order will have to do.

BALLAS: Well, then, we must try to talk them into accepting it. Mr. P., let's go.
(They turn to leave. GROSS stops them.)

GROSS: Just a moment, Mr. Ballas.

BALLAS: Yes, Mr. Gross?

GROSS: Do you know anything about a new language?

BALLAS: I think I've heard about it. I seem to recall Mr. Pillar told me about it some time ago, didn't you, Mr. P.?
(PILLAR nods.)

GROSS: Do you also recall who ordered its introduction into our organization?

BALLAS: Who was it, Mr. P., do you know?
(PILLAR shrugs.)

GROSS: Mr. Ballas. You are my deputy, aren't you?

BALLAS: Yes.

GROSS: Well then. I didn't order it. So it could only have been you.

BALLAS: One gives so many orders every day, one can't be expected to remember them all.

GROSS: Don't you realize you ought to consult me on such matters?

6

BALLAS: We didn't want to bother you with trifles.

GROSS: Actually, why is it being introduced?

BALLAS: As a sort of experiment. It's supposed to make office communications more accurate and introduce precision and order into their terminology. Am I putting it correctly, Mr. P.?
(PILLAR *nods.*)

GROSS: Was it ordered from above?

BALLAS: Not directly—

GROSS: To tell you the truth, I'm far from happy about it. You'll have to find some way to stop the whole thing at once. We don't want to be somebody's guinea pig, do we?
(HANA *re-enters by B.D. with a bottle of milk.*)

HANA *(to BALLAS)*: Good morning. *(She puts bottle on her desk, opens it, drinks, then continues combing her hair.)*

BALLAS: All right, I'll cancel my directive, and try to retrieve all the Ptydepe texts sent out so far, and have them translated back into natural language.
(To HANA:) Good morning.

GROSS: Kindly do that.

BALLAS: We don't want to be somebody's guinea pig, do we?

GROSS: Exactly.

BALLAS: Mr. P., let's go.
(They leave by S.D. GROSS crosses to Hana's desk, reaches for her milk bottle.)

GROSS: May I?

HANA: Yes, of course, Mr. Gross.

GROSS *(drinks, returns to his desk, sits down. Pause.)*: Strange relationship between those two.

HANA: I know a great many particulars about it.

GROSS: I don't want to hear them! They're both exceptionally good workers. The rest is not my business. *(Pause. Again stares at his letter. Then turns to HANA:)* Thank God, I've nipped it in the bud. Did they seriously think anybody would want to learn this gibberish?

7

HANA: Special Ptydepe classes have been set up for all departments.

GROSS: Indeed! Anybody joined them?

HANA: Everybody except you, Mr. Gross.

GROSS: Really?

HANA: It was an order.

GROSS: Whose order?

HANA: Mr. Ballas's.

GROSS: What! He didn't tell me anything about that! *(Pause.)* Anyway, I fail to see how our staff could be expected to use this Ptydepe when most of them couldn't possibly have learned it yet.

HANA: That's why a Ptydepe Translation Center has been set up. But it's supposed to be only temporary, until everybody has learned Ptydepe. Then it'll become the Ptydepe Reference Center. May I go and get the rolls?

GROSS: Well, well! A Translation Center! Where on earth did they find room for it all?

HANA: The Translation Center is on the first floor, room six.

GROSS: But that's the Accounts Department!

HANA: The Accounts Department has been moved to the cellar. May I go and get the rolls?

GROSS: Also on his order?

HANA: Yes.

GROSS: That's too much!

HANA: May I go and get the rolls?

GROSS: Run along.

(HANA pulls a string bag from her shopping bag and leaves by B.D. GROSS again does not notice when BALLAS and PILLAR enter by S.D. BALLAS coughs.)

GROSS: Now what?

BALLAS: Mr. Gross, I'm afraid you'll have to give us the order in writing, after all.

GROSS: I'll do nothing of the sort.

BALLAS: It'd be in your own interest.

GROSS: What do you mean—in my own interest?

8

BALLAS: If you'll give it to us in writing, you'll greatly
simplify the work of our clerical staff. They won't
have to fill out a special voucher to go with each
incoming letter, you see. And in view of the rumors
which have lately been circulating among them,
it would certainly be a good tactical move on your
part. Am I not right, Mr. P.?
(PILLAR *nods.*)

GROSS: What rumors?

BALLAS: Oh, about that unfortunate rubber stamp.

GROSS: Rubber stamp? What rubber stamp?

BALLAS: Apparently during the last inventory it tran-
spired that you're in the habit of taking the bank
endorsement stamp home for your children to
play with.

GROSS: That's ridiculous. Of course I have taken that
particular rubber stamp home a few times. But not
as a plaything. There are nights when I have to
take my work home to get it all done.

BALLAS: You don't have to explain it to us, Mr. Gross.
But you know how people are!

GROSS: And you think this bit of paper you want would
smooth things over?

BALLAS: I'll guarantee you that.

GROSS: All right then. As far as I'm concerned, have
it typed, and I'll sign it.

BALLAS (*at once produces a typed sheet of paper, un-
folds it, and places it on Gross' desk*): Here you
are, Mr. Gross.
(GROSS *signs.*)

BALLAS (*snatches the document and quickly folds it*):
Thank you, Mr. Gross. We thank you very much in
the name of our whole organization.
(BALLAS *and* PILLAR *are about to leave.*)

GROSS: Mr. Ballas.

BALLAS: Yes, Mr. Gross?

GROSS: Have you canceled the introduction of
Ptydepe?

BALLAS: Not yet.

9

GROSS: Why not?

BALLAS: Well, you see, we've been waiting for the right
moment. There doesn't seem to be the right sort
of atmosphere among the authorities for this move
just now. We wouldn't like it to be used against us
in any way, would we, Mr. P.?
(PILLAR shakes his head.)

GROSS: That's just an excuse.

BALLAS: Mr. Gross, you don't believe us and we're hurt.

GROSS: You've by-passed me. You've moved the Accounts
Department to the cellar.

BALLAS: That's only half the truth!

GROSS: What's the other half?

BALLAS: That I've ordered a ventilator to be installed
in the cellar next year. Mr. P., speak up, didn't I
give such an order?
(PILLAR nods.)

GROSS: What about the light?

BALLAS: The temporary accountant has brought a
candle from her home.

GROSS: Le.'s hope so!

BALLAS: Mr. P., speak up! She did bring a candle,
didn't she?
(PILLAR shrugs.)

BALLAS: Mr. P. doesn't seem to know about it. But
she did! You can go and see for yourself.

GROSS: Be that as it may, you by-passed me. You
organized Ptydepe classes, you set up a Ptydepe
Translation Center, and you made the study of
Ptydepe obligatory for all staff members.

BALLAS: Outside their working hours!

GROSS: That's beside the point.

BALLAS: Mr. Gross, I fully agree that I may not by-pass
you in things concerning the activity of our staff
during their working hours. But as for anything
outside those hours, I believe I can do as I please.

GROSS: I don't quite know what answer to give you
at this moment, but I'm sure there is a fitting
one somewhere.

10

BALLAS: Perhaps there is, perhaps there isn't. In any case, at this point we're not concerned with anything but the good of our organization. Are we, Mr. P.?
(PILLAR *nods.*)

BALLAS: Naturally, we hold the same critical attitude toward Ptydepe that you do, Mr. Gross. Only we think that if, before the inevitable collapse of the whole campaign, we can manifest certain limited initiative, it'll be of great help to our whole organization. Who knows, this very initiative may become the basis on which we might be granted that snack bar which we have been trying to get for so long. Imagine that our staff would no longer have to travel all that way on their coffee break.

GROSS: All right. It's quite possible that in this way we might indeed get the snack bar. This, however, in no way changes the fact that you've by-passed me a number of times and that, lately, you've been taking far too many decisions on your own authority.

BALLAS: I? I beg your pardon! Haven't we just been consulting you about such a trifle as a new incoming-mail book? You're not being fair to us, Mr. Gross. You're not at all fair.

GROSS: Mr. Ballas, let me make a suggestion.

BALLAS: Yes?

GROSS: Let's be quite blunt with each other for a while, shall we? It'll simplify the situation a great deal and speed up the clarification of our points of view.

BALLAS: Shall we accept, Mr. P.?
(PILLAR *nods.*)

BALLAS: I accept.

GROSS: Why did you say that you hold a critical attitude toward Ptydepe and that you're only interested in the snack bar, when in fact you believe in Ptydepe and do everything you can to get it quickly introduced?

BALLAS: Matter of tactics.

GROSS: A little shortsighted.

BALLAS: I wouldn't say so.

GROSS: It never occurred to you that sooner or later I'd see through your tactics?

BALLAS: We knew you'd create obstacles and therefore we arranged it so you wouldn't see what we were after until we were strong enough to surmount your obstacles. There's nothing you can do to stop us now. The overwhelming majority of our staff stands resolutely behind us, because they know that only Ptydepe can place their work on a truly scientific basis. Isn't that so, Mr. P.?
(PILLAR *nods.*)

GROSS: You seem to forget that it is I who bear the full responsibility for our organization, I in whom the trust has been placed. Thus, it is up to me to judge what is good for our organization, and what is not. So far it is I who am the Managing Director here.

BALLAS: We cannot ignore the stand of the masses. The whole organization is seething and waiting for your word.

GROSS: I won't be dictated to by a mob.

BALLAS: You call it a mob, we call it the masses.

GROSS: You call it the masses, but it is a mob. I'm a humanist and my concept of directing this organization derives from the idea that every single member of the staff is human and must become more and more human. If we take from him his human language, created by the centuries-old tradition of national culture, we shall have prevented him from becoming fully human and plunge him straight into the jaws of self-alienation. I'm not against precision in official communications, but I'm for it only in so far as it humanizes Man. In accordance with this my innermost conviction I can never agree to the introduction of Ptydepe into our organization.

BALLAS: Are you prepared to risk an open conflict?

GROSS: I place the struggle for the victory of reason

12

and of moral values above a peace bought by their loss.

BALLAS: What do you say to this, Mr. P.?
(PILLAR shrugs in embarrassment.)

GROSS: I suggest to you that we all forget what has just happened between us and that we part in peace before I'm forced to take the whole matter seriously. *(A short pause. HANA enters by B.D., carrying a string bag full of rolls, puts it into her shopping bag, sits down and begins to comb her hair.)*

BALLAS *(turns to PILLAR)*: It seems he's not yet ripe for realistic discussion. We've overrated him. Never mind. Let's give him—*(looks at his watch)*—what do you say, an hour?
(PILLAR nods.)

BALLAS: Time is on our side. An hour from now we'll no longer be handling him with kid gloves. The patience of the masses is great, but it is not infinite. He'll be sorry. Let's go.
(They leave by S.D.)

GROSS: Unheard of! *(Sits down, notices his memorandum, stares at it, turns to HANA.)* Hana!

HANA: Yes, Mr. Gross?

GROSS: Do you know Ptydepe?

HANA: No.

GROSS: Then how did you know this was an official memorandum?

HANA: They say that in the first stage Ptydepe was used only for important official memoranda and that these are now being received by some of the staff.

GROSS: What are these memos about?

HANA: They are supposed to inform the recipients about decisions based on the findings of the last audit in their departments.

GROSS: Indeed? What sort of decisions?

HANA: All sorts, it seems. Very positive and very negative ones.

GROSS: Damn that rubber stamp! Where on earth did you learn all this?

13

HANA: Oh, in the dairy shop this morning.

GROSS: Where did you say the Translation Center is?

HANA: First floor, room six. To get to it one must go through the Ptydepe classroom.

GROSS: Ah yes! Former Accounts Department. Well, I'm off to lunch. *(Takes his memorandum from his desk and hurries out B.D.)*

HANA *(calls after him)*: You'll like it, Mr. Gross. They have goose in the canteen today!

SCENE 2

The Ptydepe classroom. Teacher's desk in the back-
ground; in the foreground five chairs. LEAR *is standing*
behind his desk, lecturing to four CLERKS *who are seated*
with their backs to the audience. Among them is THUMB.

LEAR: Ptydepe, as you know, is a synthetic language,
    built on a strictly scientific basis. Its grammar is
    constructed with maximum rationality, its vocabu-
    lary is unusually broad. It is a thoroughly exact
    language, capable of expressing with far greater
    precision than any current natural tongue all the
    minutest nuances in the formulation of important
    office documents. The result of this precision is of
    course the exceptional complexity and difficulty
    of Ptydepe. There are many months of intensive
    study ahead of you, which can be crowned by
    success only if it is accompanied by diligence, per-
    severance, discipline, talent and a good memory.
    And of course, by faith. Without a steadfast faith
    in Ptydepe, nobody yet has ever been able to learn
    Ptydepe. And now, let us turn briefly to some of
    the basic principles of Ptydepe. The natural lan-
    guages originated, as we know, spontaneously, uncon-
    trollably, in other words, unscientifically, and their
    structure is thus, in a certain sense, dilettantish.
    As far as official communications are concerned,
    the most serious deficiency of the natural languages
    is their utter unreliability, which results from the
    fact that their basic structural units—words—are
    highly equivocal and interchangeable. You all know

that in a natural language it is often enough to ex-
change one letter for another (goat—boat, love—
dove), or simply remove one letter (fox—ox), and
the whole meaning of the word is thus changed.
And then there are all the homonyms! Consider
what terrible mischief can be caused in inter-office
communications when two words with entirely
different meanings are spelled exactly the same way.
P-o-s-s-u-m. Possum—possum. The first, designating
an American small arboreal or aquatic nocturnal
marsupial mammal with thumbed hind-foot—
(THUMB *giggles.*)

LEAR: The second, the Latin equivalent of "I am able."
Such a thing is quite unthinkable in Ptydepe. The
significant aim of Ptydepe is to guarantee to every
statement, by purposefully limiting all similarities
between individual words, a degree of precision, re-
liability and lack of equivocation, quite unattainable
in any natural language. To achieve this, Ptydepe
makes use of the following postulation: if similarities between any two words is to be minimized,
the words must be formed by the least probable
combination of letters. This means that the creation of words must be based on such principles
as would lead to the greatest possible redundancy
of language. You see, a redundancy—in other words,
the difference between the maximum and the real
entropy, related to the maximum entropy and ex-
pressed percentually—concerns precisely that super-
fluity by which the expression of a particular piece
of information in a given language is longer, and
thus less probable (i.e., less likely to appear in this
particular form), than would be the same expression
in a language in which all letters have the same prob-
ability of occurrence. Briefly: the greater the redundancy of a language, the more reliable it is, because the smaller is the possibility that by an ex-
change of a letter, by an oversight or a typing error,
the meaning of the text could be altered.

(GROSS enters by B.D., his memorandum in hand, crosses the room and leaves by S.D.)

LEAR: How does, in fact, Ptydepe achieve its high redundancy? By a consistent use of the so-called principle of a sixty per cent dissimilarity; which means that any Ptydepe word must differ by at least sixty per cent of its letters from any other Ptydepe word of the same length (and, incidentally, any part of such a word must differ in the same way from any Ptydepe word of this length, that is from any word shorter than is the one of which it is a part). Thus, for example, out of all the possible five-letter combinations of the 26 letters of our alphabet—and these are 11,881,376—only 432 combinations can be found which differ from each other by three letters, i.e., by sixty per cent of the total. From these 432 combinations only 17 fulfill the other requirements as well and thus have become Ptydepe words. Hence it is clear that in Ptydepe there often occur words which are very long indeed.

THUMB *(raising his hand)*: Sir—

LEAR: Yes?

THUMB *(gets up)*: Would you please tell us which is the longest word in Ptydepe? *(Sits down)*

LEAR: Certainly. It is the word meaning "a wombat," which has 319 letters. But let us proceed. Naturally, this raises the question of how Ptydepe solves the problem of manageability and pronounceability of such long words. Quite simply: inside these words the letters are interspersed with occasional gaps, so that a word may consist of a greater or smaller number of so-called subwords. But at the same time the length of a word—as indeed everything in Ptydepe—is not left to chance. You see, the vocabulary of Ptydepe is built according to an entirely logical principle : the more common the meaning, the shorter the word. Thus, for example, the most commonly used term so far known—that is the term "whatever"—is rendered in Ptydepe by the word "gh."

As you can see, it is a word consisting of only two letters. There exists, however, an even shorter word—that is "f"— but this word does not yet carry any meaning. I wonder if any of you can tell me why. Well?

(Only THUMB *raises his hand.)*

LEAR: Well, Mr. Thumb?

THUMB *(gets up)*: It's being held in reserve in case science should discover a term even more commonly used than the term "whatever."

LEAR: Correct, Mr. Thumb. You get an A.

SCENE 3

The Secretariat of the Translation Center. It is something between an office and a waiting room. A large desk, a typist's desk, a few straight chairs or armchair, a small conference table. STROLL is seated on it, a paper bag full of peaches in his lap. He is consuming them with gusto. GROSS enters by B.D., his memorandum in hand.

GROSS: Good morning.

STROLL *(with his mouth full)*: Morning.

GROSS: I've dropped in to get acquainted with the activities of the Translation Center. I'm the Managing Director.

STROLL *(with his mouth full)*: So you're the Managing Director?

GROSS: Yes. Josef Gross.

STROLL *(slowly lets himself down from the table, finishes his peach, wipes hands on handkerchief and walks over to GROSS)*: Very glad to meet you. Sorry I didn't recognize you. I've been here only a very short time and so I still haven't met everybody. My name's Stroll. Head of the Translation Center. Do sit down.
(STROLL folds his handkerchief and shakes hands with GROSS. Both sit down. STROLL lights a cigarette. GROSS tries all his pockets, but cannot find his.)

STROLL: Everything here is still so to speak at the diaper stage.

GROSS: I understand.

19

STROLL: We're still grappling with a great many teething troubles.

GROSS: That's clear enough—

STROLL: It's no easy matter, you know.

GROSS: No, quite.

STROLL: Tell me, exactly what would you like to find out?

GROSS: I'd like to see how you've organized the process of making translations. Do you do them while one waits?

STROLL: We'll make a translation from Ptydepe while you wait for any member of our organization who is a citizen of our country and has an authorization to have a Ptydepe text translated.

GROSS: Does one need a special authorization?
(SAVANT enters by S.D.)

SAVANT: Morning, Otto. Have you heard that there's goose for lunch today?

STROLL *(jumps up)*: What! Did you say goose?

SAVANT: That's what the chaps in the Secretariat said. Pick you up on the way to the canteen, right?

STROLL: Right! The sooner the better!
(SAVANT leaves by S.D.)

STROLL: I love goose, you know! Now, what were we talking about?

GROSS: You were saying that one needs an authorization to get a translation made.

STROLL: Right. Well now, look here. We, the staff, do use Ptydepe, but we're no experts. Let's face it, we're no linguists, are we? So, naturally, the exploitation and development of Ptydepe cannot be left in our hands alone. If it were it might lead to unwelcome spontaneity and Ptydepe might quite easily change under our very noses into a normal natural language and thus lose its whole purpose. *(Suddenly he halts, becomes preoccupied, then quickly gets up.)* Excuse me. *(Hurries out by S.D.)*
(GROSS stares after him in surprise, then begins another search through his pockets, but finds

20

no cigarettes. Pause. HELENA *enters by S.D.)*

HELENA: Was Alex here?

GROSS: I don't know who that is.

HELENA: You're not part of this shop, love?

GROSS: On the contrary. I'm Managing Director.

HELENA: Are you, love? Well, you must do something about this snack bar, I mean it! It's a bloody shame to see our girls traipse miles for a cup of tea, it really is. Does anyone think about people in this shop?

GROSS: And who, may I ask, are you?

HELENA: I'm the chairman. But you can call me Nellie.

GROSS: The chairman of what, if you'll forgive my asking?

HELENA: Of what? Don't know of what just yet. As a matter of fact we're having a meeting about that very thing this afternoon. But I'm already so bloody busy I don't know which way to turn. They don't give you time to have a proper look around and they expect you to start cleaning up their smelly little messes straight away. Well, see you. *(Leaves by S.D.)* *(Pause. GROSS again tries his pockets. Then looks at his watch. Waits. Pause. STROLL at last returns by S.D. Walks slowly. Buttons up his trousers while walking.)*

STROLL: You don't like goose?

GROSS: I do. You were saying that Ptydepe cannot be left only in your hands.

STROLL: Right. And that's why every department which starts to introduce Ptydepe is assigned a special methodician, a so-called Ptydepist, who, being a specialist, is supposed to ensure that Ptydepe gets used correctly.

(MARIA enters by B.D., carrying a string bag full of onions.)

MARIA *(walking toward S.D.)*: Good morning.

GROSS: Good morning.

(MARIA leaves by S.D.)

STROLL: Our Ptydepist fulfills this task by issuing for
every translation a special authorization—

MARIA *(off-stage)*: Here are the onions, Miss Helena.

STROLL: Which enables him to record all outgoing
translations from Ptydepe.

HELENA *(off-stage)*: Would you mind putting them over
by the filing cabinet, that's a good girl.

STROLL: Thus he obtains all the necessary material for
various statistics, on the basis of which he then directs
the use of Ptydepe.
*(MARIA returns by S.D., carrying an empty string
bag, puts it in the drawer, sits at typist's desk and
begins to work.)*

GROSS: So, if I've understood you correctly, you'll give
a translation only to those staff members who can produce an authorization from your Ptydepist.

STROLL: Right.
(SAVANT enters by S.D., knife and fork in hand.)

SAVANT: Are you ready?

STROLL *(to MARIA)*: Where are my tools?
*(MARIA takes knife and fork from a drawer and
hands them to him.)*

GROSS: Who is your Ptydepist?

STROLL: Have they been washed?

MARIA: Of course.

STROLL *(to GROSS)*: What did you say?

GROSS: Who is your Ptydepist?

STROLL: Dr. Savant here.

GROSS *(shakes hands with SAVANT)*: How do you do.
I'm Josef Gross, the Managing Director.

SAVANT: How do you do. I'm Alex Savant, the Graduate
Ptydepist. My degree is like a doctorate, you know.

GROSS: I'd like a word with you, Dr. Savant.

STROLL: Are you going to ask for breast?

SAVANT: Sorry, Mr. Gross, but we really must go and
have our lunch now. Shouldn't want to miss it.
(To STROLL:) I prefer a leg.
*(SAVANT and STROLL leave by B.D. GROSS
stands for a while in surprise, then slowly sits down.*

Pause. He looks at his watch. Waits. Again looks at his watch, puts it to his ear. Then tries all his pockets.)

GROSS: Have you a cigarette, by any chance?

MARIA: I'm sorry, I don't smoke.
(Pause. GROSS again looks at his watch. Then he notices a box on the desk.)

GROSS: What's that?

MARIA: Cigars.

GROSS: May I take one?

MARIA: Oh no! They belong to Mr. Stroll. He's counted them. He'd be very angry if you did.
(Long pause. GROSS stretches, looks at his watch, finally gets up, slowly approaches MARIA and peers over her shoulder to see what she is doing.)

MARIA: Reports—

GROSS: Mmnn—
(GROSS slowly walks around the office, examining everything, then again sits down. HELENA quietly enters by S.D. GROSS sits with his back toward her. HELENA gestures to MARIA to keep quiet. Tiptoeing, she creeps up to GROSS and from behind puts her hands over his eyes. GROSS starts.)

HELENA *(changing her voice to make it sound like a man's)*: Guess who?

GROSS: I beg your pardon!

HELENA: Guess who!

GROSS: Take your hands off at once!

HELENA: Come on, guess! Who am I?

GROSS *(hesitates a moment)*: The District Inspector.

HELENA: No.

GROSS: The Regional Inspector.

HELENA: No.

GROSS: The Inspector General.

HELENA: No.

GROSS: Ilon.

HELENA: No.

GROSS: Then it's Karel.

23

HELENA: No—no—no.

GROSS: Do stop it, Ilon! You're being very silly!

HELENA: Shall I tell you?

GROSS: Would you, please!

(HELENA *takes her hands away.* GROSS *turns.*)

HELENA: You're not Alex? Sorry, love. I thought it was Alex Savant. Hasn't he showed up yet?

GROSS: What charming manners!

MARIA: He's gone to lunch.

HELENA *(to GROSS)*: Starchy, aren't you? What the hell! It was just a bit of fun, that's all. Well, see you. *(Leaves by S.D.)*

(Pause. GROSS once more tries his pockets.)

GROSS: Have you a cigarette, by any chance?

MARIA: You've already asked, Mr. Gross.

GROSS: I'm sorry, I must have forgotten.

(GROSS looks at his watch, puts it to his ear, begins to be impatient. Again the same search, then gets up and wanders about the office. Stops behind MARIA and peers over her shoulder to see what she is doing.)

MARIA: Reports—

GROSS: Mmnn—

(Pause. GROSS again notices Stroll's box, slowly approaches, looks at it for a while, opens it quietly, takes a cigar, smells it. MARIA watches him. GROSS realizes he is being watched, replaces the cigar and returns to his seat. Pause.)

GROSS *(loudly)*: Good God! It wouldn't hurt him, would it?

(STROLL and SAVANT are returning by B.D. in lively conversation, they hand their knives and forks to MARIA, then sit down.)

STROLL: That was simply delicious. The way it was cooked! Straight through!

SAVANT: I think it was better last time.

STROLL: Not juicy enough. The very best was the time before last.

GROSS: Dr. Savant—

STROLL *(to MARIA)*: Would you go and see if Mr. Langer is having his lunch today? If not, ask whether he'd mind sending me his voucher.

GROSS: Dr. Savant—

(MARIA quickly walks out by B.D. SAVANT watches her with greedy appreciation.)

SAVANT *(turning to GROSS)*: Not bad, eh?

GROSS: Rather pleasant.

SAVANT: Sexy little thing, isn't she?

GROSS: Dr. Savant—

STROLL: Her? Sexy? Come off it!

SAVANT *(to GROSS)*: Yes?

GROSS: I understand you can authorize the making of a translation from Ptydepe.

SAVANT: Yes, for those who bring me their documents.

GROSS: What do you mean? What sort of documents?

SAVANT: Personal registration.

(STROLL offers a cigarette to SAVANT.)

SAVANT *(taking it)*: Ta.

(STROLL and SAVANT light their cigarettes. GROSS again tries his pockets, hesitates, then speaks up.)

GROSS: I'm sorry—er—could you sell me a cigarette?

STROLL: I wish I could, but I've only three left.

GROSS: Oh, I see. I'm sorry. *(To SAVANT:)* Why do you actually need the personal registration documents?

SAVANT *(to STROLL)*: She is sexy, you know. Just wait till someone catches her in the dark! *(To GROSS:)* What did you say?

GROSS: Why do you actually need the personal registration documents?

SAVANT: Well, it's like this, you see. Although I've been employed by this organization, I'm no common or garden staff member. I am, as you well know, a scholar of a new sort, of course, as everything about Ptydepe is new. And as such I naturally take certain— shall we say—exceptions to some of the rather bureaucratic procedures of my staff colleagues. As a matter

25

of fact, it's not really exceptions I take—it's more like objections. No, objections isn't the right word either. How shall I put it? I'm sorry. You see, I'm used to speaking in Ptydepe and so it's rather difficult for me to find the right words in a natural language.

GROSS: Please go on.

SAVANT: In Ptydepe one would say axajores. My colleagues sometimes ylud kaboz pady el too much, and at the same time they keep forgetting that etrokaj zenig ajte ge gyboz.

STROLL: Abdy hez fajut gagob nyp orka?

SAVANT: Kavej hafiz okuby ryzal.

STROLL: Ryzal! Ryzal! Ryzal! Varuk bado di ryzal? Kabyzach? Mahog? Hajbam?

SAVANT: Ogny fyk hajbam? Parde gul axajores va dyt rohago kabrazol? Fabotybe! They think they can simply send me a chap, I'll give him an O.K., and that'll be the end of it. Byzugat rop jů ge tyrak! If our statistics are to make any sense at all we must have concrete foundations to build on. We must have detailed information about everybody who comes in contact with Ptydepe, in order to get the greatest possible variety of sociological and psychological data.

GROSS: Wouldn't it be enough if a chap just told you himself everything you want to know about him?

SAVANT: That wouldn't guarantee that everything was hutput.

GROSS: I beg your pardon?

SAVANT: Hutput. Quite exact.

(MARIA returns by B.D.)

MARIA: I'm sorry, but it appears that Mr. Langer will definitely be eating his lunch today.

STROLL: Pity.

(MARIA sits at her desk and continues working.)

GROSS: Excuse me, you were speaking about the uncertainties of verbal statements.

SAVANT: Ah, yes! Well now, all the particulars concerning each employee have long been recorded with the greatest precision and without any possible subjective zexdohyt—I'm sorry—point of view—

GROSS: I understand—*(Jokingly.)* I've a completely hutput zexdohyt of it.

SAVANT: Zexdohyttet! You've forgotten that every noun preceded by the adjective hutput takes on the suffix "tet"—

STROLL: Or tete.

SAVANT: Or tete. Quite. Many people make this mistake. Even Mr. Wassermann in one of his letters—

GROSS: Excuse me, you were speaking about the advantages of the personal registration documents.

SAVANT: Ah, yes! Well now, the personal registration documents often record things which even the particular employee doesn't know about himself. *(To* STROLL:*)* Nuzapom?

STROLL: Zapom. Yd nik fe rybol zezuhof.

SAVANT: Yd nik—yd nek.

GROSS: To sum up. You'll authorize a translation only for those members of the staff who can produce their documents. All right, where does one get them?

(HELENA enters by S.D.)

HELENA: Hallo everybody!

SAVANT *(sings)*: Hallo everybody hallo—

HELENA: You know whose birthday it is? Eddi Kliment's!

SAVANT: Eddi's? Is it?

HELENA: There's a do going on for him next door. So drop everything and come along. *(To* MARIA:*)* Seems the grocer's got limes. Would you mind running over and getting me eight?

(MARIA hurries out by B.D.)

SAVANT: What are they drinking?

HELENA: Vodka.

SAVANT: Did you hear that, Otto?

(SAVANT and STROLL hasten toward the S.D.)

GROSS: You haven't told me yet where one gets those documents.

27

SAVANT: Why, right here from our chairman. From
    Nellie, of course.
    (SAVANT and STROLL quickly walk out by S.D.
    HELENA is about to follow them.)
GROSS: Miss Helena—
HELENA *(halts by the door)*: What?
GROSS: I'd like a word with you.
HELENA: Later, love. You'll have to wait.
GROSS: Here?
HELENA: Where else?
GROSS: You mean you don't mind leaving me here
    alone? With all the classified material and all
    that?
HELENA: You won't be alone, love. There's a chink in
    the wall. You're being watched by our Staff
    Watcher.
GROSS: Good gracious! A chink?
HELENA: Wouldn't be much good if he was actually in
    here. That way he'd be able to watch only one of-
    fice, wouldn't he? This way he can watch five of
    them at once. You see, his cubicle is surrounded by
    offices and each is furnished with an observation
    chink. So all he has to do is to walk—at random,
    watch—from one to another and peer.
GROSS: Interesting idea.
HELENA: Isn't it, love? And it's my idea, too! My point
    was to stop visitors from having to hang about in
    the hall when the office is empty. Bloody nuisance,
    isn't it? Even in these piddling details one must be
    thinking of the good of the people! Well, see you.
    (Runs out S.D.)
    (GROSS wanders about investigating the walls.)
GEORGE *(after a while off-stage)*: Don't bother. The
    chink is well disguised.
GROSS: I should say it is! One might make use of this
    idea in other departments as well.
GEORGE *(off-stage)*: Not likely. This kind of thing has
    to be planned for by the architect from the very
    start.

GROSS: I see what you mean. On the other hand, he couldn't very well have planned for it here.

GEORGE *(off-stage)*: He didn't. He made a mistake in his calculations. And when this building was erected it was found that there was this space left over between the offices. So it was used in this way.

GROSS: A really stimulating idea!
(Pause. GROSS sits down, looks impatiently at his watch, gets up, sits down, again looks at his watch, gets up, searches his pockets, again sits down. MARIA runs in by B.D.)

GROSS: What's the matter?

MARIA: Forgot my purse. *(Opens drawer of typing desk and rummages in it hastily.)*

GROSS: Miss—

MARIA: Yes?

GROSS: Do you know Ptydepe?

MARIA: A bit.

GROSS: Can you translate it?

MARIA: I'm strictly forbidden to make any translations before I've passed my exams.

GROSS: But on my authority you might try to make a translation, mightn't you? It doesn't have to be perfect, you know.
(MARIA smiles.)

GROSS: What's so funny about it?

MARIA: You wouldn't understand. It's impossible, that's all.

GROSS: What's your name?

MARIA: Maria.

GROSS: Maria! A pretty name.

MARIA: Do you like it?

GROSS: Very much. Maria—just for once! Nobody'll know about it.

MARIA: Mr. Gross! Somebody might walk in any minute. Please be reasonable!

GROSS *(urgently)*: Go on, sweetheart!

MARIA: And what about the Staff Watcher?

GROSS *(whispers)*: You could whisper the translation to me.

29

MARIA: The limes will soon be sold out and Miss Helena will be angry. 'Bye. *(Having found her purse, she runs out by B.D.)*
(Pause. GROSS, tired, sinks into his chair. He stares ahead, mechanically begins to try his pockets again. Then gets up and walks straight to the cigar box. When he is about to open it, he quickly takes his hand away and looks around cautiously.)

GROSS: Mr. Watcher—*(Pause.)* Mr. Watcher—*(Pause.)* Listen, Mr. Watcher, can you hear me? Have you got a cigarette? *(Pause.)* He must have fallen asleep. *(Carefully opens the box.)*

GEORGE *(off-stage)*: What do you mean—fallen asleep!

GROSS *(jerks away from the box)*: Well, why didn't you answer me?

GEORGE *(off-stage)*: I wanted to test you out.

GROSS: I beg your pardon! Do you realize who I am? The Managing Director!

GEORGE *(off-stage)*: Habuk bulugan.

GROSS: I beg your pardon?

GEORGE *(off-stage)*: Habuk bulugan, avrator.

GROSS: What did you mean by that?

GEORGE *(off-stage)*: Nutuput.

GROSS *(looks at his watch, then walks quickly to B.D., turns by the door)*: I won't put up with any abuse from you! I expect you to come to me and apologize. *(Exit by B.D.)*

GEORGE *(off-stage)*: Gotroch!

SCENE 4

*The Director's office. BALLAS and PILLAR are silently
waiting for GROSS. PILLAR has a notebook in his hand.
HANA is combing her hair. Then GROSS hurries in by
B.D., crosses to his desk, sits down with studied casual-
ness. For a while there is menacing silence.*

BALLAS: Well?

GROSS: Well?

BALLAS: The hour has passed. Ready to be more
    sensible now?

GROSS: Certainly not.

BALLAS: As you may have noticed, the introduction of
    Ptydepe into our organization successfully proceeds.
    What are you going to do about it?

GROSS: Put a stop to it.

HANA: Mr. Gross, may I go and get the chocolates?

BALLAS: How?

GROSS: By issuing an order that the introduction of
    Ptydepe be stopped and its use cancelled.

BALLAS: You cannot.

GROSS: Why not?

BALLAS: You never issued any order for its intro-
    duction and use, so you're in no position to stop
    and cancel anything at all.

GROSS: Then you'll do it.

BALLAS: I haven't issued any such order either. Have
    I, Mr. P.?
    (PILLAR shakes his head.)

HANA: Mr. Gross, may I go and get the chocolates?

GROSS: What do you mean?

31

BALLAS: It was just a verbal directive, based on an as-
surance that you'd validate it by a supplementary
order.

GROSS: Then I'll simply not give any supplementary
order.

HANA: Mr. Gross, may I go and get the chocolates?

BALLAS: The introduction of Ptydepe is in full swing
and it will naturally go on even without it. *(To
HANA:)* Run along.
*(HANA immediately stops combing her hair and
is off by B.D.)*

GROSS: In that case I'll have to report the whole matter
to the authorities.

BALLAS *(laughs)*: Did you hear that, Mr. P.? He doesn't
know that the authorities have taken a great fancy
to Ptydepe.

GROSS: If that's the case, why haven't they made its
use obligatory in all organizations?

BALLAS: Playing it safe. If Ptydepe succeeds, they'll
have plenty of time to take the credit for it, if it
fails, they'll be able to dissociate themselves from
it and blame the departments.

GROSS: I hope you don't expect me to be a traitor to
my beliefs.

BALLAS: I do.

GROSS: How do you propose to make me?

BALLAS *(points at Pillar's book)*: Do you see this book?
Not long ago it was improperly authenticated by
your order, although it had not been registered
by the Purchasing Department and thus was your
own property. Do you know what that constitutes?
Abuse of authority.

GROSS: Good God! Don't you make yourself sick?

BALLAS: Do we make ourselves sick, Mr.P.?
(PILLAR shakes his head.)

BALLAS: Of course we don't. When the good of Man is
at stake, nothing will make us sick.

GROSS: But you yourself got me to sign it!

BALLAS: I did? I don't seem to remember—

32

GROSS: By your hints about the rumors concerning that damned rubber stamp!

BALLAS: I wouldn't bring that up, if I were you.

GROSS: Why not?

BALLAS: Because it's no extenuating circumstance at all. Just the reverse, in fact.

GROSS: I don't know what you're talking about.

BALLAS: Don't you? Well, look here. If it weren't for the rubber stamp affair, you might have claimed that you signed the authentication of this book moved by a sincere desire to help our clerical staff, which of course wouldn't have excused your conduct, but would at least have explained it somewhat on humanitarian grounds; while if you do bring up this motive now, you'll be admitting thereby that you signed it moved merely by petty cowardice, so as to silence legitimate inquiries into the circumstances of the rubber stamp affair. Do you follow me? If, on the other hand, you hadn't signed it, you might have pretended that you were indeed taking the rubber stamp home for reasons of work, but your signature proves that you were clearly aware of your guilt. As you see, both your errors are intertwined in such an original way that the one greatly multiplies the other. By publicizing the circumstances which you consider extenuating you would leave nobody in any doubt whatever about the real motives of your conduct. Well then, shall we come to an agreement?

GROSS: All right, I'll resign.

BALLAS: But we don't want you to.

GROSS: Well, what do you want me to do?

BALLAS: Sign the supplementary order for the introduction and the use of Ptydepe in our organization.

GROSS: But you said, didn't you, that Ptydepe will be used even without a supplementary order? Then why do you insist on it now?

BALLAS: That's our business.

(A long pause.)

GROSS *(quietly)*: Are you sure that Ptydepe will really make office communications more precise?

BALLAS: I'm glad our discussion is at last reaching a realistic level. Mr. Pillar, would you offer Mr. Gross some milk?

(PILLAR hands GROSS Hana's bottle of milk. GROSS drinks mechanically.)

BALLAS: Look here. You yourself know best how many misunderstandings, suspected innuendos, injustices and injuries can be contained in one single sentence of a natural language. In fact, a natural language endows many more-or-less precise terms, such as for example the term "colored," with so many wrong, let's say emotional, overtones, that they can entirely distort the innocent and eminently human content of these terms. Now tell me sincerely, has the word "mutarex" any such overtones for you? It hasn't, has it? You see! It is a paradox, but it is precisely the surface inhumanity of an artificial language which guarantees its truly humanist function! After Ptydepe comes into use, no one will ever again have the impression that he's being injuried when in fact he's being helped, and thus everybody will be much happier.

(HANA returns by B.D., carrying a box of chocolates, puts it in her shopping bag, sits down and once more begins to comb her hair. Pause.)

GROSS: You have convinced me. Have the supplementary order for the introduction of Ptydepe in our organization typed and bring it to me for signature.

BALLAS: Mr. Gross, we're overjoyed that you've grasped the demands of the times. We look forward to our further work in this organization under your expert and enlightened leadership. *(He takes out a sheet of paper and puts it on the desk in front of GROSS.)* Here is the typed order you request.

(GROSS signs. When he finishes, BALLAS and PILLAR begin to applaud. GROSS also claps uncertainly a few times. They all shake hands and

34

congratulate each other. Finally, BALLAS *takes the signed document.)*

BALLAS: Well, that's that. Aren't you hungry, Mr. P.?
   (PILLAR shakes his head. Pause.)
BALLAS: I believe that from now on we'll be working very closely together.
GROSS: We'll have to. Without your help it'd probably be rather hard for me to find my bearings in the new situation. Perhaps at the beginning we shan't be able to avoid directing the organization, so to speak, hand in hand.
BALLAS: I have a better idea. What about me being the director and you my deputy. Won't that make things much easier?
GROSS *(confused)*: But you said, didn't you, that you were looking forward to working under my expert and enlightened leadership?
BALLAS: You will be able to use your expertise and enlightenment just as well as a deputy. I'll go and get my things, while you, Mr. Gross, will kindly move out of my desk!
GROSS: As you wish, Mr. Ballas.
BALLAS: Mr. P., let's go.
   (BALLAS and PILLAR leave by S.D. GROSS collects his papers from his desk and stuffs them in his pockets, then carefully takes down the fire extinguisher hanging on the wall.)
GROSS: Things do seem to be moving rather fast.
HANA: Mr. Gross—
GROSS: There was nothing else I could do. An open conflict would have meant that I'd be finished. This way—as Deputy Director—I can at least salvage this and that.
HANA: Mr. Gross—
GROSS: Anyway, who knows, maybe this—Ptydepe— will turn out to be a good thing after all. If we grasp the reins firmly and with intelligence—
HANA: Mr. Gross—
GROSS: What is it?

35

HANA: May I go and get my lunch?

GROSS: Run along!

> (HANA *hastily takes her knife and fork, and hurries out by B.D. BALLAS and PILLAR enter by S.D. BALLAS is carrying a fire extinguisher, identical with the one GROSS just took off the wall. GROSS halts in the center and sadly stares ahead.)*

GROSS *(to himself)*: Why can't I be a little boy again? I'd do everything differently from the beginning.

> *(GROSS lingers dejectedly for a second longer, then turns and slowly walks out by the B.D., the fire extinguisher clasped in his arms. Meanwhile, BALLAS has placed his own extinguisher in the emptied space, PILLAR has taken various papers from his pockets and spread them on the desk. Then they both sit down at the desk, make themselves comfortable, grow still, look at each other and smile happily.)*

SCENE 5

The Ptydepe classroom. Again LEAR *lecturing to four*
CLERKS.

LEAR: Historically, the natural languages originated in all
    probability through the development of the inarticu-
    late shrieks by which a primitive creature expressed
    his basic reactions to the surrounding world. The
    very oldest group of words is thus the interjections.
    At the same time, the interjections form an unus-
    ually easy part of Ptydepe, which is quite obvious,
    as their frequency in inter-office communications
    is rather limited. This is why the interjections will
    form the first few lessons of your curriculum. Well
    then, let us proceed to the interjections. As you
    know, every word of a natural language—including
    the interjections—has several Ptydepe equivalents,
    which differentiate its several shades of meaning.
    To start with, for each interjection we shall learn
    only one, the most common, expression in Ptydepe.
    Nevertheless, as an example, I'd like to demon-
    strate to you through the Ptydepe renderings of
    the interjection "boo," how rich and precise is
    Ptydepe, even in this marginal sphere.
    (GROSS enters by B.D., fire extinguisher in his
    arms, walks toward the S.D., hesitates, halts,
    thinks for a moment, then turns to LEAR.)
GROSS: Sir—
LEAR: What is it?
GROSS: I do hate to interrupt you, but I happen to have
    with me a little Ptydepe text, and I was wondering

if—just as a refresher, you know—it might not be a good thing to acquaint our colleagues here with the actual shape of Ptydepe. Perhaps if you read it aloud and then possibly translated it, it might be of interest to the class.

LEAR: As regards a sample of an actual Ptydepe text, I've prepared my own, authorized, specimen. However, for the sake of variety, I'm quite prepared to read your text as well, that is, provided you can show that your interest in Ptydepe is vital and you're not just trying to interfere with the class. You may sit down.

(GROSS, *surprised, mechanically sits in an empty chair, puts the extinguisher in his lap.)*

LEAR: Generally speaking, the interjection "boo" is used in the daily routine of an office, a company, a large organization when one employee wants to sham-ambush another. In those cases where the endangerment of an employee who is in full view and quite unprepared for the impending peril is being shammed by an employee who is himself hidden, "boo" is rendered by "gedynrelom." The word "osonfterte" is used in substantially the same situation when, however, the imperiled employee is aware of the danger. "Eg gynd y trojadus" is used when an employee who has not taken the precaution, or the time, or the trouble to hide wants to sham-ambush another employee who is also in full view, in case it is meant as a joke. "Eg jeht kuz" is used in substantially the same situation when, however, it is meant in earnest. "Ysiste etordyf" is used by a superior wishing to test out the vigilance of a subordinate. "Yxap tseror najx" is used, on the contrary, by the subordinate toward a superior, but only on the days specially appointed for this purpose.

And now let me see if you've been paying attention. Who can tell us how one says "boo" in Ptydepe when a hidden employee wants to sham-ambush another employee who is in full view and quite unprepared for the danger? Mr. Thumb!

THUMB *(gets up)*: Gedynrelom. *(Sits down.)*

LEAR: Correct. And when the imperiled employee is aware of the danger? *(Points at GROSS.)*

GROSS *(gets up)*: Danger menacing an employee who is in full view?

LEAR: Yes.

GROSS: Who is aware of the danger?

LEAR: Yes.

GROSS: And the perpetrator is hidden?

LEAR: Yes.

GROSS: Aha—yes—I see. Well—in that case one says— damn it, it was on the tip of my tongue.

LEAR: Mr. Thumb, do you know?

THUMB *(gets up)*: Osonfterte. *(Sits down.)*

LEAR: There you are. You see how easy it is! Well, let's take another case, shall we? For example, how would a superior say "boo" when he wishes to test out the vigilance of a subordinate?

GROSS: A superior?

LEAR: Yes.

GROSS: The vigilance of a subordinate?

LEAR: Yes.

GROSS: I say, I think I know this one!

LEAR: Well, then tell us.

GROSS: We're translating the interjection "boo," aren't we?

LEAR: Yes.

GROSS: I'm sure I know it—only—it has sort of slipped my mind.

LEAR: Well, Mr. Thumb?

THUMB *(gets up)*: Ysiste etordyf. *(Sits down.)*

LEAR: Correct, Mr. Thumb. Well, shall we try once more? Third time never fails, eh? Let's see if you can tell us, for example, how does an employee who has not taken the precaution, or the time, or the trouble to hide say "boo" if he wants to sham-ambush another employee

39

who is also in full view, when it is meant in earnest?

GROSS: I'm afraid I don't know.

LEAR: Let me help you. Eg—

GROSS: Eg—eg—eg—

LEAR: Jeht—

GROSS: Yes, I do remember now. Eg jeht.

LEAR: Wrong. Mr. Thumb, would you mind telling him?

THUMB *(gets up)*: Eg jeht kuz. *(Sits down.)*

LEAR: Correct. Eg jeht doesn't mean anything at all. Those are only two sub-words of the word eg jeht kuz.

GROSS: The third sub-word escaped me.

LEAR: Unfortunately, the first two sub-words also escaped you, like all the other Ptydepe words which I was trying to teach you only a moment ago. When one considers that the interjections are the easiest part of Ptydepe and that my requirements have indeed been minimal, one cannot avoid concluding that in your case it is not merely a matter of average inattentiveness or negligence, but of that particular inability to learn any Ptydepe whatsoever which stems from a profound and well-disguised doubt in its very sense. Under these circumstances I don't see why I should oblige you by reading aloud and, what's more, translating an unauthorized text. Chozup puzuk bojt!

GROSS: Goodness! So much fuss about three little words! *(Clasps fire extinguisher in his arms and leaves by S.D.)*

LEAR: Let us proceed. Mr. Thumb, can you tell us how a subordinate says "boo" to a superior in Ptydepe on the days specially appointed for this purpose?

THUMB *(gets up)*: Yxap tseror najx. *(Sits down.)*

LEAR: Correct, Mr. Thumb. You get an A.

SCENE 6

The Secretariat of the Translation Center. The office is empty, only the noise of a party going on off-stage can be heard: gay voices, laughter, clinking of glasses, singing of "Happy birthday to you," drinking songs, etc. During the first part of the following scene the noise occasionally becomes very loud, then quiets down a little. GROSS hurries in by B.D. with fire extinguisher still in his arms, halts in the center, looks around, listens, then he puts extinguisher on the floor and tentatively sits down. MARIA enters by B.D., carrying a paper bag full of limes and walks toward S.D. GROSS gets up at once.

GROSS: Good afternoon.

MARIA: Good afternoon. *(Leaves by S.D. Off-stage:)* Here are the limes, Miss Helena.

HELENA *(off-stage)*: Would you mind putting them down by the coat rack? That's a good girl. *(MARIA re-enters by S.D., sits at her desk and begins to work.)*

GROSS *(also sits down)*: Miss Helena is next door?

MARIA: Yes. They're celebrating Mr. Kliment's birthday.

GROSS: Do you think she'd mind coming here for a moment?

MARIA: I'll ask—*(Exits by S.D. Returns after a short while.)* Mr. Gross—

GROSS: Yes?

MARIA: You're no longer the Managing Director?

GROSS: I'm his deputy now.

41

MARIA: Oh! Forgive me for asking—but what happened?

GROSS: Oh, well, we just—we exchanged jobs, Mr. Ballas and I.

MARIA: Well, Deputy Director is also a very responsible position.

GROSS: It is, isn't it? As a matter of fact, to some extent it's even more responsible than the director's! I can remember, for instance, that when I was the director, my deputy often solved some of the most important problems for me. Will Miss Helena come?

MARIA: You'll have to wait a little, I'm afraid.

(HELENA looks in at S.D. GROSS quickly gets up.)

HELENA *(to MARIA)*: Come here a moment, will you?

(MARIA leaves with HELENA by S.D. GROSS slowly sits down again. Long pause. Loud voices and noise from next door. After a while all quiets down.)

GROSS: Mr. Watcher—

GEORGE *(off-stage)*: What is it?

GROSS: We're friends again, aren't we?

GEORGE *(off-stage)*: Oh, well—why not?

(Pause. Noise of the party.)

GROSS: Mr. Watcher—

GEORGE *(off-stage)*: What now?

GROSS: Aren't you celebrating?

GEORGE: I'm following the party through the chink.

GROSS: Does it look like being a long one?

GEORGE *(off-stage)*: They've finished the vodka.

GROSS: Have they?

(Pause. Singing off-stage, changing into cheers.)

VOICES *(off-stage)*:

> For he's a jolly good fellow
> For he's a jolly good fellow
> For he's a jolly good fellow
> Which nobody can deny.

Hip—hip—hurrah!

(Cheers and shouts culminate in laughter which, however, soon dies down, voices are beginning to recede, a few farewells, then all is quiet. The party is over. STROLL and SAVANT

42

enter by S.D., absorbed in animated conversation.)

STROLL: I bet she was shy!

SAVANT: To start with. But then—

STROLL: Then what?

SAVANT: You know what.

STROLL: Come off it! I bet you've made up that part about xachaj ybul!

SAVANT: Absolutely not! Literal truth! Down to the last letter.

STROLL: Come off it.

SAVANT: Mind you, if it hadn't been for kojufer bzal gaftre, we'd have certainly luhofr dyboroch!

STROLL: Does she actually—

SAVANT: I'm telling you. She's a wild 'un! *(Sings:)* Cigarettes and whisky and wild wild women—

STROLL: How old is she?

SAVANT: Sixteen.

STROLL: I prefer them a teency weency bit younger.

HELENA *(enters by S.D.)*: Come on, everybody! Let's have some coffee!

STROLL: That's a thought! Where's Maria?

SAVANT: Our sexy little thing? Mr. Gross might know.

GROSS: I?

SAVANT: Don't try to deny it! You lust after her!

GROSS: I beg your pardon!

SAVANT: You called her sweetheart. The Staff Watcher heard you.

GEORGE *(off-stage)*: You talk too much, Alex.

SAVANT: Listen, why don't you shut up and do your watching!

STROLL: Now, now, friends! *(Calls:)* Maria!

SAVANT *(sings)*: Maria—Maria—Maria!

HELENA: Leave her alone, love. She's ironing my slip. I'll make the coffee. *(Calls toward S.D.:)* Where do you keep the percolator?
(MARIA runs in by S.D., iron in one hand, with the other she takes percolator from drawer, and runs out again.)

43

STROLL: You won't mind, Mr. Gross, will you, if we
    don't offer you any coffee? We've very little left,
    you see. It'll just about make three cups.
GROSS: Never mind. I don't really care for any.
STROLL: Nellie, Mr. Gross doesn't care for any coffee.
    Make it three cups, but make a double one for me,
    will you? *(To* SAVANT*:)* I say, what about a
    cigar with the coffee?
SAVANT: That's a thought!
GROSS: Miss Helena—
HELENA *(calling toward S.D.)*: Where do you keep the
    coffee?
    *(MARIA runs in by S.D. with the iron, takes tin of
    coffee from another drawer, runs out again. Mean-
    while STROLL has taken cigar box off his desk.
    Offers one to SAVANT.)*
GROSS: Miss Helena—
STROLL: That's what I call a cigar!
SAVANT *(takes one)*: Ta.
    *(STROLL also takes one. Both light them expertly.
    GROSS watches them. As usual, he first tries all
    his pockets, then takes out some money and offers
    it to STROLL.)*
GROSS: Excuse me—may I—if you'd—
STROLL: Sorry, Mr. Gross, I wouldn't recommend it.
    I really wouldn't. They're awfully heavy, you're
    not used to them, they're sure to make you cough.
GROSS: Just one—
STROLL: I mean it. You'd be making a mistake.
    *(GROSS , disappointed, puts his money back.
    STROLL and SAVANT smoke with gusto.)*
GROSS: Miss Helena—
HELENA: Why don't you call me Nellie, love?
    What is it?
GROSS: Miss Nellie, do you issue the documents one
    needs to get a translation authorized?
STROLL: Goose, vodka, and a cigar, that's what I call
    living.
SAVANT: And what a cigar!

GROSS: I said, do you issue the documents one needs to get a translation authorized?

HELENA *(calling toward S.D.)*: Where do you get water?

MARIA *(off-stage)*: I'll get it. *(Runs in by S.D., iron in hand, grabs kettle, and runs out B.D.)*

HELENA *(to GROSS)*: What?

GROSS: Do you issue the documents one needs to get a translation authorized?

HELENA: Yes. To anybody who hasn't received a memo written in Ptydepe.

GROSS: Why?

SAVANT: Downright heady!

STROLL: I should say!

GROSS: I said, why?

HELENA *(calling toward S.D.)*: Where do you keep the cups?

MARIA *(off-stage)*: Coming! *(Runs in by S.D., carrying iron and kettle full of water. Pours water into percolator, takes out cups and a spoon, hands them to HELENA, and runs out by S.D.)*

HELENA *(spoons out coffee into percolator)*: Why what?

GROSS: Why this condition?

HELENA: Because I cannot be expected to give the documents of personal registration to every Tom, Dick, and Harry without making damned sure they don't conflict with the findings of the last audit in his blessed memo!

GROSS: Why can't you look at his memo and see what it says?

STROLL: Poor Zoro Bridel used to smoke only these. And he was a real gourmet!

SAVANT: Pity he passed away!

GROSS: I said, why?

HELENA *(calling toward S.D.)*: Sugar!

(MARIA runs in, carrying iron, hands HELENA a paper bag of sugar and again runs out.)

HELENA *(to GROSS)*: Why what?

GROSS: Why can't you look at his memo and see what it says?

45

HELENA: I'm forbidden to translate any Ptydepe texts.
   (Toward S.D.:) It's almost empty.
MARIA *(off-stage)*: There's another bag in the drawer.
GROSS: Good gracious! What can a staff member do in
   such a case?
SAVANT: Mr. Bidel loved goose, didn't he?
STROLL: Zoro? Simply mad about it!
HELENA *(calling toward S.D.)*: Water's boiling.
   (MARIA runs in by S.D., puts iron on floor, un-
   plugs percolator, pours coffee into cups.)
HELENA *(to GROSS)*: What?
GROSS: What can a staff member do in such a case?
HELENA: He can have his memo translated. Listen
   everybody! Today your coffee's hyp nagyp!
   (MARIA passes cups to STROLL, SAVANT, and
   HELENA, then takes iron and runs out S.D.)
SAVANT: Nagyp avalyx?
HELENA: Nagyp hayfazut!
   (STROLL, SAVANT, and HELENA pass the spoon
   around, offer sugar to each other, sip their coffee
   with gusto, absorbed in their Ptydepe conversation.
   GROSS, growing more and more desperate, turns
   from one to the other.)
GROSS: Mr. Stroll—
STROLL: Hayfazut gyp andaxe. *(To GROSS:)* Yes?
SAVANT: Andaxe bel jok andaxu zep?
GROSS: In order to make a translation from Ptydepe,
   you require an authorization from Mr. Savant—
HELENA: Andaxe zep.
STROLL: Ejch tut zep. Notut?
GROSS: Dr. Savant—
SAVANT: Tut. Gavych ejch lagorax. *(To GROSS:)* Yes?
HELENA: Lagorax nagyp.
GROSS: In order to grant the authorization, you require
   the documents from Miss Helena?
STROLL: Lagorys nabarof dy Zoro Bridel cef o abagan.
SAVANT: Mavolde abagan?
GROSS: Miss Helena—
HELENA: Abagan fajfor! *(To GROSS:)* Yes?

46

STROLL: Fajfor? Nu rachaj?

GROSS: In order to issue the documents, you require that a staff member have his memorandum translated.

SAVANT: Rachaj gun.

HELENA: Gun znojvep?

STROLL: Znojvep yj.

SAVANT: Yj rachaj?

HELENA: Rachaj gun!

STROLL: Gun znojvep?

SAVANT: Znojvep yj.

HELENA: Yj rachaj?

STROLL: Rachaj gun!

SAVANT: Gun znojvep?

GROSS *(shouts)*: Quiet!

(At once all three become silent and quickly get up. Not on account of GROSS, of course, but becaue BALLAS and PILLAR have just quietly entered by B.D. Gross' back is turned toward BALLAS and PILLAR, thus he does not see them.)

GROSS: I'm the Deputy Director and I insist that you show me some respect! You may sit down.
(Naturally they remain standing. Pause. MARIA, unaware of what has been happening, enters by S.D., carrying the ironed slip over her arm. Seeing the situation, she crumples the slip behind her back and stands like the others.)

GROSS: As I've just discovered, any staff member who has recently received a memorandum in Ptydepe can only be granted a translation of a Ptydepe text after his memorandum has been translated. But what happens if the Ptydepe text which he wishes translated is precisely that memorandum? It can't be done, becaue it hasn't yet been translated officially. In other words, the only way to learn what is in one's memo, is to know it already. An extraordinary paradox, when you come to think of it. Ladies and gentlemen, do you come to think of it? I ask you, what must an employee of our organization—whoever he may be—do in order to escape this vicious, vicious circle?

(For a second there is dead silence.)

BALLAS: He must learn Ptydepe, Mr. Gross. *(To the others:)* You may sit down.

(They all sit down at once. MARIA, *still hiding the slip behind her, runs fearfully to her desk.)*

GROSS *(faintly)*: Are you here?

BALLAS: Yes, we are.

GROSS: Have you been here long?

BALLAS: Not long.

GROSS: I didn't hear you come in.

BALLAS: We entered quietly.

GROSS: Excuse me, I—

BALLAS: There are things, Mr. Gross, that cannot be excused. And when, at the very time in which the whole organization is conducting a courageous struggle for the introduction and establishment of Ptydepe, an official, referring to the activities of our employees, speaks with such malicious innuendo and mean irony about—I quote—"a vicious, vicious circle," then it cannot be excused at all.

GROSS: I'm sorry, Mr. Ballas, but the circumstance I've allowed myself to point out is simply a fact.

(Long pause.)

GROSS *(in a quiet, broken voice)*: I plead guilty. I acknowledge the entire extent of my guilt, while fully realizing the consequences resulting from it. Furthermore, I wish to enlarge my confession by the following self-indictment. I issued an illegal order which led to the fraudulent authentication of my own, personal notebook. By this action I abused my authority. I did this in order to avert attention from the fact that I'd appropriated a bank endorsement stamp improperly for my private use. I request for myself the most severe punishment.

BALLAS: I think that under these circumstances it is

48

no longer possible for him to remain in our organization. What do you say, Mr. P?
(PILLAR shakes his head.)

BALLAS: Certainly not. Come to my office tomorrow
morning. We'll settle the formalities connected with
your dismissal. *(Calls:)* George, come out of there!
You'll be my deputy. *(To the others:)* You may
leave now. Mr. P., let's go.
*(BALLAS and PILLAR leave by B.D., STROLL,
SAVANT, and HELENA by S.D. GROSS remains
standing in the center. Motionless, he stares ahead.
MARIA watches him in silence. It seems she would
like to help him in some way. Then she takes the
cigar box and shyly offers one to GROSS. GROSS
does not see her. HELENA looks in at S.D.)*

HELENA *(to MARIA)*: Seems the grocer's got fresh
cantaloupes. Would you mind running over and
getting me ten? If you're quick about it, I'll give
you a taste!
*(HELENA disappears. MARIA hastily replaces cigar
box, snatches her string bag and runs out B.D.
GROSS hangs his head, takes the fire extinguisher,
and slowly, sadly leaves by B.D. Just then a small
secret door opens in one of the side walls and
GEORGE backs out of it on all fours. When he
is quite out, he straightens, stretches, arranges
his clothes with a dash of vanity, takes a cigar from
the box and haughtily struts out by B.D.)*

INTERVAL

49

SCENE 7

*The Director's office. BALLAS and PILLAR enter by
B.D., take off their coats, sit at the desk. BALLAS begins to go through the morning mail, like GROSS at the
beginning of the play. One letter suddenly arrests his
attention, he glares at it, then starts to read it aloud.*

BALLAS *(reads)*: Ak ok utuh d utoked yle umobert
ehusome, ragedv dy, orts uner re kyrg ydnek, vylaz
edyvz uzed, ladnyvk ref unyked yles — *(Puts down
the letter, hesitates, turns to* PILLAR:*)* You don't
know Ptydepe, do you?
(PILLAR shakes his head.)
BALLAS: You might have learned it by now!
STROLL *(looks in at S.D.)*: I hope I'm not interrupting.
(To PILLAR :*)* Ferry, would you come here a
moment?
*(PILLAR gets up at once and leaves with STROLL
by S.D. BALLAS looks after them in surprise.
Meanwhile GROSS quietly enters by B.D., fire
extinguisher clasped in his arms.)*
BALLAS *(to himself)*: Ferry?
*(BALLAS, puzzled, shakes his head, then again
stares at his letter. GROSS after a while speaks up
timidly.)*
GROSS: Good morning.
BALLAS: You're here?
GROSS: I haven't been here long.
BALLAS: What do you want?
GROSS: I was supposed to come to your office today con-
cerning my dismissal from our organization, Mr. Ballas.

50

BALLAS: I'm busy now. Come back in a while—

GROSS: Sorry. Thank you. I'll come later.

    (GROSS quickly backs out by B.D. PILLAR returns by S.D. and sits at his place.)

BALLAS: What did he want?

    (PILLAR gestures that it was nothing important. BALLAS shakes his head doubtingly, and again stares at his letter. HANA enters by B.D., wearing a coat and carrying a vast shopping bag.)

HANA: Good morning.

BALLAS *(without looking up)*: Morning.

    (HANA hangs coat on coat rack, sits at her desk and begins to comb her hair. After a moment, BALLAS turns to her.)

BALLAS: Hana—

HANA: Yes, Mr. Ballas?

BALLAS: You know Ptydepe, don't you?

HANA: I'm sorry, I don't.

BALLAS: Why not? I thought you'd been going to the Ptydepe classes.

HANA: I used to, but I had to give them up. May I go and get the milk?

BALLAS: Why?

HANA: It was too hard for me. May I go and get the milk?

BALLAS: Aren't you ashamed? The secretary to the Managing Director and Ptydepe's too hard for her!

HANA: May I go and get the milk?

BALLAS: Run along.

    (HANA takes milk bottle and hurries out by B.D.)

BALLAS: I hope you won't end up like her!

    (PILLAR makes an embarrassed face.)

SAVANT *(looks in at S.D.)*: Morning, Jan! Can you spare Ferry a minute?

BALLAS: By all means—

SAVANT: Ta. Cheerio!

    (SAVANT gestures to PILLAR. PILLAR gets up at once and both leave by S.D. BALLAS looks angrily after them. Meanwhile GROSS

quietly enters by B.D., extinguisher in his arms.)

BALLAS *(to himself)*: Ferry! Ferry! Ferry! *(Again stares at his letter.)*

GROSS: Good morning.

BALLAS: You're here again?

GROSS: You said, Mr. Ballas, that I should come back in a while.

BALLAS: By which I didn't mean such a short while!

GROSS: Sorry. I'll come later. Sorry—*(He is backing toward B.D.)*

BALLAS: Listen—

GROSS: Yes, Mr. Ballas?

BALLAS: Nothing.

GROSS: Did you want something?

BALLAS: No, no. You may go.

(GROSS backs out by B.D. PILLAR returns by S.D. and sits down at his place.)

BALLAS: What did he want?

(PILLAR puts on a vague expression.)

BALLAS: I don't like the way they keep addressing you. Much too familiar.

(PILLAR shrugs, embarrassed. HANA returns by B.D., drinks, then continues combing her hair. Pause.)

BALLAS *(to HANA)*: Is Ptydepe so difficult to learn?

HANA: It makes great demands on one's memory, Mr. Ballas.

BALLAS: Others can learn it—

HANA: Very few can, Mr. Ballas. Most of the staff have had to give it up.

BALLAS: Even when all give up, you should persevere!

HANA: But you also dropped out, Mr. Ballas, after the first lesson.

BALLAS: That's different. I had to interrupt my studies for reasons of work. You think it's child's play to be at the helm of this colossus? And, what's more, in these times? Come and try it and you'd see.

HANA: But Ptydepe really makes great demands on

people. Besides, they say it's based on doubtful
principles. May I go and get the rolls?

BALLAS: Who says that?

HANA: Mr. Pillar here.

BALLAS: Surely not Mr. Pillar! And if, by any chance,
he did say such a thing, it was just in fun. Who of
the staff actually knows Ptydepe?

HANA: Only the teacher and the personnel of the
Translation Center. May I go and get the rolls?

BALLAS: Run along.
*(HANA takes string bag and leaves by B.D. As soon
as she is out, BALLAS turns furiously against
PILLAR.)*

BALLAS: You talk too much! Far too much!

HELENA *(looks in by S.D.)*: Hallo everybody! Ferry,
love—would you?
(PILLAR gets up at once.)

HELENA: Well, see you.
*(HELENA and PILLAR leave by S.D. BALLAS
jumps up furiously. He does not notice that
GROSS has again entered with his fire extinguisher
by B.D.)*

BALLAS *(to himself)*: I'll teach you a lesson! Ferry!
*(BALLAS sits down. Again stares at his letter.
Pauses. Then GROSS speaks up.)*

GROSS: Good morning.

BALLAS: You're here again?

GROSS: You said, Mr. Ballas, that I should come back
in a while.

BALLAS: By which I didn't mean such a short while!

GROSS: Sorry. I'll come later. Sorry—*(He is backing
toward B.D.)*

BALLAS: Listen—

GROSS: Yes, Mr. Ballas?

BALLAS: Nothing.

GROSS: Did you want something?

BALLAS: I just wanted to say that I seem to have over-
done it a bit yesterday. You know, there were so
many people about, I wasn't sure who might be

among them—my nerves were a bit ruffled after
all that happened—

GROSS: Thank you. You're very kind. Thank you. But
the dismissal stands, doesn't it?

BALLAS: Dismissal? Well, for the moment, perhaps
we needn't take such drastic measures. You can't
be my deputy, of course—

GROSS: Of course—

BALLAS: But there is an opening.

GROSS: Is there? To do what?

BALLAS: The position of Staff Watcher has become
free.

GROSS: Do you think I could handle it?

BALLAS: Well, why don't you give it a try for a while?
We'll see how it works out.

GROSS: Very kind of you, Mr. Ballas. When may I
start?

BALLAS: At once, if you like.

GROSS: Thank you, Mr. Ballas. Thank you very much.
(GROSS *backs out by B.D.* PILLAR *returns by S.D.
and sits down at his place.*)

BALLAS: What did she want?
(PILLAR *puts on a vague expression.*)

BALLAS: Don't you play games with me!
(HANA *returns by B.D., her string bag full of rolls.
She puts them in her shopping bag, sits down and
combs her hair.*)

BALLAS (*to* HANA): Who else says that Ptydepe is
based on doubtful principles?

HANA: All except you, Mr. Ballas.

BALLAS: Don't exaggerate!

HANA: Really.

BALLAS: What else do they say?

HANA: That it's only a matter of time before you find
it out too.

BALLAS: Indeed. This is the reward one gets for
all one has done for them! (*Hands his letter to
HANA.*) Couldn't you at least make out what
this is about?

HANA *(skims the letter)*: It could be either a memo-
    randum concerning the last audit—
BALLAS: Hardly—
HANA: Or a protest.
BALLAS: What sort of protest?
HANA: I don't know.
BALLAS: Why should it be a protest, of all things?
HANA: It's being rumored that protests written in Ptydepe
    get preferential treatment.
BALLAS: Where did you hear all this?
HANA: Oh, in the dairy shop this morning.
BALLAS: If anybody thinks he can come and protest
    here, I'll—I'm off to lunch. *(He grabs his letter
    and leaves by B.D.)*
HANA *(calls after him)*: You'll like it, Mr. Ballas. They
    have goulash in the canteen today!

The Ptydepe classroom. All is as before, with the exception that LEAR *is lecturing to only one clerk,* THUMB. *All other chairs are empty.*

LEAR: And now I shall name, just for the sake of pre-
     liminary orientation, some of the most common
     Ptydepe interjections. Well then, our "ah!" be-
     comes "zukybaj," our "ouch!" becomes "bykur,"
     our "oh!" becomes "hayf dy doretob," English
     "pish!" becomes "bolypak juz," the interjection of
     surprise "well!" becomes "zyk," however, our "well,
     well!" is not "zykzyk," as some students erroneously
     say, but "zykzym"—
     *(GROSS with his fire extinguisher enters by B.D.,
     crosses the room and leaves by S.D.)*
LEAR: "Aow!" becomes "varylaguf yb de solas," or
     sometimes, though much more rarely, "borybaf,"
     "bang!" as the symbol of a shot or explosion be-
     comes "hetegyx ujhoby," "bang" as a colloquial
     expression for sudden surprise is "maluz rog." Our
     "eek!" becomes "hatum"—
THUMB *(raises his hand)*: Sir—
LEAR: What is it?
THUMB *(gets up)*: Would you mind telling us how one
     says "oops" in Ptydepe?
LEAR: "Mykl."
THUMB: Thank you. *(Sits down.)*
LEAR: "Psst!" becomes "cetudap," "mmnn" becomes
     "vamyl," the poetic "oh!" is rendered in Ptydepe by
     "hrulugyp." The "hoooo" of a ghost is translated

mostly as "lymr," although I'd prefer the expression "mryb uputr." Our very important "hurrah!" becomes in Ptydepe 'frnygko jefr dabux altep dy savarub goz texeres." And now a little test of your memory. Aow?

(THUMB *raises his hand.*)

LEAR: Mr. Thumb!

THUMB (*gets up*): Varylaguf yb de solas. (*Sits down.*)

LEAR: Eek?

(THUMB *raises his hand.*)

LEAR: Mr. Thumb!

THUMB (*gets up*): Hatum. (*Sits down.*)

LEAR: Psst?

(THUMB *raises his hand.*)

LEAR: Mr. Thumb!

THUMB (*gets up*): Cetudap. (*Sits down.*)

LEAR: Bang?

THUMB: As the symbol of a shot?

LEAR: No, as the colloquial expression for sudden surprise.

(THUMB *raises his hand.*)

LEAR: Mr. Thumb!

THUMB (*gets up*): Maluz rog.

LEAR (*correcting his pronunciation*): Maluz—

THUMB: Maluz—

LEAR: M—a—l—u—z—

THUMB: M—a—l—u—z—

LEAR: Listen carefully: m—a—l—u—z—

THUMB: M—a—l—u—z—

LEAR: Your pronunciation isn't too good. How do you say well?

THUMB: Zyk.

LEAR: And well, well?

THUMB: Zykzyk.

LEAR: Zykzym!!

THUMB: I'm sorry, I forgot.

LEAR: Mr. Thumb! Mr. Thumb! Yippee!

THUMB: We haven't learned yippee yet, sir.

LEAR: Don't try to excuse yourself. You simply don't

know it. Hurrah!

THUMB: Frnygko jefr dabux altep dy savarub gop texeres.

LEAR: Goz texeres!!

THUMB: I mean, goz texeres.

LEAR: Such an important word! No, no, Mr. Thumb! It won't work this way. I've placed so many hopes in you, and you have what? Well? You have disappointed me! Yes, disappointed! No, no, this way we can't do what? Well? Carry on. Certainly not. This way our class would soon turn into what? Well? Go on, answer me!

THUMB: I don't know.

LEAR: Then try.

THUMB: A kindergarten?

LEAR: No.

THUMB: A borstal?

LEAR: No.

THUMB: Bedlam?

LEAR: Quite correct! Bedlam! No, no! Under these circumstances I can't let you carry on with your studies. You'd only slow down the class and hold up the other students. Please leave the classroom! *(THUMB takes his briefcase and sadly leaves by B.D.)*

LEAR *(addressing the empty classroom)*: Let us proceed. "Hallo!" becomes "trevunt," "gosh!" is translated as "kavlyz ubahaj kupit," the American "gee!" becomes "hofro gaborte," "pooh!" is translated as —

SCENE 9

The Secretariat of the Translation Center. The room is empty, then MARIA *enters by B.D., carrying a string bag full of onions, crosses the room and leaves by S.D.*

MARIA *(off-stage)*: Here are the onions, Miss Helena.
HELENA *(off-stage)*: Would you mind putting them
    by the filing cabinet? That's a good girl.
    (MARIA returns by S.D., carrying an empty string
    bag, sits at the typist's desk and works for a
    while, then looks about her a few times, takes a
    mirror from drawer, props it up in front of her,
    carefully takes out a new hat and tries it on in
    front of the mirror.)
GROSS *(off-stage)*: It suits you.
    (MARIA starts, tears the hat off her head, shoves
    it hastily into the drawer, hides the mirror, and
    fearfully looks about.)
GROSS *(off-stage)*: Don't worry. It's only me, Gross.
MARIA *(heaves a sigh of relief)*: Oh! But where are
    you?
GROSS *(off-stage)*: I'm the Staff Watcher now.
MARIA: You? Oh, no!
GROSS *(off-stage)*: Yes, Mr. Ballas dropped my dismissal
    and he's letting me work here for a trial period.
MARIA: You? Staff Watcher?
GROSS *(off-stage)*: Very much so. And in the given
    circumstances it really seems the best solution for
    me. I only wish I could get used to the lack of
    space.
MARIA: Goodness! And I've found a job for you.

GROSS *(off-stage)*: Have you? What sort of job?

MARIA: With a theater group.

GROSS *(off-stage)*: But I can't act.

MARIA: You could always manage a bit part. There's always bit parts cropping up, you know, a butler, a messenger, a workman, that sort of thing. Well, anyway, if worst came to worst you could prompt the actors.

GROSS *(off-stage)*: Yes, perhaps. Are you somehow connected with the theater?

MARIA: My brother works with this group.

GROSS *(off-stage)*: You're kind. *(Pause.)* Maria—

MARIA: Yes?

GROSS *(off-stage)*: Isn't it odd? I have to look at you all the time.

MARIA: Oh, Mr. Gross!

HELENA *(looks in at S.D.)*: Seems the grocer's got limes. Would you mind running over and getting me eight? *(Disappears.)*
(MARIA takes string bag from drawer and runs out by B.D. Short pause, then BALLAS stalks in energetically by B.D., his letter in hand. Looks about, tries his pockets, but finds no cigarettes. Turns toward secret door.)

BALLAS: Are you there?

GROSS *(off-stage)*: But of course, Mr. Ballas.

BALLAS: Well, how goes it?

GROSS *(off-stage)*: Very well, thank you.

BALLAS: Many strangers?

GROSS *(off-stage)*: Only three visitors in number five.

BALLAS: Alone in the office?

GROSS *(off-stage)*: One, for a moment.

BALLAS: Behaved?

GROSS *(off-stage)*: Decently.

BALLAS: Good. I think you'll manage. Anything else?

GROSS *(off-stage)*: Sorry, but what else, precisely?

BALLAS: Well, for example, what sort of things are being said about Ptydepe among the staff?

60

(Pause.)

GROSS *(off-stage)*: I'm sorry, Mr. Ballas, but I—how should I put it?—I—I'm not an—you know what I mean.

BALLAS: I know. You still haven't shaken off the shackles of outdated prejudice. But you must understand that it's for a good cause. What's more, it is, in a certain sense, your moral duty.

(STROLL enters by S.D. and swiftly walks toward B.D.)

BALLAS *(to STROLL)*: Just a moment!

(STROLL halts.)

BALLAS *(toward secret door)*: Is that quite clear?

GROSS *(off-stage)*: Quite clear, Mr. Ballas.

BALLAS *(to STROLL)*: I say, old boy! How goes the translating?

STROLL: Very well, thank you.

BALLAS: Tell me, how many texts have you translated so far?

STROLL: Into Ptydepe or from Ptydepe?

BALLAS: Well, let's say into Ptydepe.

STROLL: One. I'm just working on the second one now.

BALLAS: So few?

STROLL: That's not so few.

(SAVANT enters by S.D. and quickly walks toward B.D.)

BALLAS *(to SAVANT)*: Just a moment!

(SAVANT halts.)

BALLAS *(to STROLL)*: Slow work, isn't it?

STROLL: Indeed it is. Every expression has several variants in Ptydepe and so one must consult the author of the submitted text regarding each separate word, in order to find out precisely how it was meant and which of the Ptydepe variants to use. Am I not right, Alex?

SAVANT: Quite right. Often the authors themselves aren't sure. They simply don't know such precision from their mother tongue.

STROLL: The shades of meaning of individual words in Ptydepe are so subtle that most of the staff

61

can't grasp them at all.

BALLAS: Why don't you get some help?

STROLL: Help? But you know how things are! Am I not right, Alex?

SAVANT: So far, nobody has really managed to learn Ptydepe. Only Pekarek, and then he left for steam-navigation.

BALLAS: Well, what you'll have to do is to speed up your translating. The world won't come to an end if an occasional little word isn't exactly right. (PILLAR *looks in at B.D. BALLAS does not see him. PILLAR stares questioningly at STROLL, who gestures to him that he is ready to go.*)

STROLL: Sorry, Mr. Ballas, I have a meeting now—

BALLAS: Well then, go along.
(PILLAR *disappears. STROLL hurries out by B.D. SAVANT is about to follow.*)

BALLAS: Wait, Alex! Just one more little thing. Tell me, how is Ptydepe actually making out? From the expert's point of view, I mean.

SAVANT: Hard to say. I still have no basis for my statistics, so I can't form any real opinion. (HELENA *enters by S.D. and briskly walks toward B.D.*)

BALLAS *(to* HELENA*)*: Just a moment!
(HELENA *halts.*)

BALLAS *(to* SAVANT*)*: What about the results in other organizations?

SAVANT: They're all right, I suppose. Except that wherever Ptydepe has started to be used more widely, it has automatically begun to assume some of the characteristics of a natural language: various emotional overtones, imprecisions, ambiguities. Correct, Nellie?

HELENA: Correct. And you know what? They say that the more one uses Ptydepe the more it gets soiled by these characteristics.

BALLAS: Did you say emotional overtones? But in that case Ptydepe is losing its very purpose!

SAVANT: One could put it that way.

(PILLAR, unnoticed by BALLAS, looks in at B.D. silently beckons to SAVANT who gestures back that he is ready.)

BALLAS: What can be done about it?

SAVANT: Practically nothing. I'm sorry, Mr. Ballas, do you mind if I go now? I have a meeting—

BALLAS: Well then, go along.

(PILLAR disappears. SAVANT hurries out by B.D. HELENA is about to follow.)

BALLAS: Wait, Nellie!

HELENA: What is it, Jan?

BALLAS: Listen, we two have always been able to talk as man to man. Now, tell me quite frankly, I mean really quite frankly, do you get the impression that Ptydepe isn't doing as well as it might be, or, to put it bluntly, that it's sort of got stuck?

HELENA: I do, love.

BALLAS: Thank you, Nellie.

(PILLAR looks in at B.D.)

HELENA: May I go now?

BALLAS: Run along.

(PILLAR disappears. HELENA runs out by B.D. BALLAS thoughtfully paces up and down. Then sits and again talks toward the secret door.)

BALLAS: Mr. Gross—

GROSS *(off-stage)*: Yes, Mr. Ballas.

BALLAS: I hope you aren't taking seriously what occurred yesterday. You do realize, don't you, it was just a bit of a show for the sake of the others? Listen, why don't I call you Jo, shall I?

GROSS *(off-stage)*: But of course, Mr. Ballas, I'll be delighted.

BALLAS: I say, old boy— come out of there! You don't want to be doing that sort of work! You! I don't see why you shouldn't carry on as my deputy.

GROSS *(off-stage)*: After what happened?

BALLAS: We must take some risks, damn it! I won't

hear of your being abused in this way, Jo! We're
having some difficulties at present. Ptydepe isn't
doing as well as it might be—

GROSS *(off-stage)*: Yes, I've heard.

BALLAS: The way things are now, I simply need you
here, Jo!

*(GROSS emerges from the secret door, scrambling
out backward on all fours.)*

BALLAS: Sit down.

(GROSS sits down.)

BALLAS: Where's the enthusiasm we all felt when we
were launching Ptydepe! I worked at it as stubbornly
as a mule! You know, drank only water, ate only
purple hearts, went without sleep, just slaved and
organized; when the cause was at stake, I was quite
ruthless. Well, you remember, don't you?

GROSS: I do remember.

BALLAS: That was the best time of my life! And now
see how it's all turned out! This isn't what we
wanted, is it?

GROSS: Well, perhaps things will mend themselves
again somehow.

BALLAS: Listen, Jo! You and I, between us, we'll
pull things together again! You have your experience,
you know how things were done in the past when
everything worked; I know how they ought to be
done so they'll work in the future; if we two work
hand in hand, I'll bet anything you like, we'll
hammer out something damn well astonishing!
Are you free tonight?

GROSS: Yes.

BALLAS: Good. Now look, let's meet quietly at some
pub, have a glass of be~   ~d really think things
out! We'll map out   ~e plan, so we know how
to go about it all. Who should I rely on here if
not on you, old boy!

GROSS: But I—

BALLAS *(cuts in)*: And now fetch George and tell him
to march back into his cubicle. He's already proved

himself in the job and he must see that what we
need now above all in the high positions is specialists.
(GROSS *leaves by B.D. Long pause. BALLAS searches
his pockets, no cigarettes. Looks at his watch. STROLL
enters by B.D., carrying a folder, and briskly walks toward S.D.)*

BALLAS: Otto!
    (STROLL *halts.)*
BALLAS: You still haven't told me about your trans-
    lations from Ptydepe.
STROLL: So far, I haven't translated anything from
    Ptydepe.
    (SAVANT *enters by B.D., carrying a folder, and
    walks toward S.D.)*
BALLAS: Alex!
    (SAVANT *halts.)*
BALLAS *(to* STROLL*)*: Why not?
STROLL: Up till now nobody has brought me any author-
    ization from Alex.
BALLAS: Alex! Why do you refuse to authorize trans-
    lations?
SAVANT: But I can't authorize them without personal
    registration documents.
    (HELENA *enters by B.D., carrying a folder, and
    walks toward S.D.)*
BALLAS: Nellie!
    (HELENA *halts.)*
BALLAS *(to* SAVANT*)*: You mean in all this time nobody
    has brought you any documents from Nellie?
SAVANT: That's right.
BALLAS: Nellie! Why do you refuse to issue those
    damned documents?
HELENA: Oh, for heaven's sake, love! I can't issue
    them until I've made sure they don't conflict with the
    findings in the memos, and I can't learn the findings
    because the blessed memos are written in Ptydepe
    and, as you bloody well know, I'm forbidden to
    make any translations whatsoever. Hasn't the girl
    brought my limes yet?

BALLAS: Then why doesn't Otto translate the memos?

STROLL: I can translate only after getting an authorization from Alex!

BALLAS: Then Alex will have to start granting the authorizations!

SAVANT: I can't, if nobody has the documents from Nellie!

BALLAS: Do you hear that, Nellie? You'll have to start giving people the documents regardless!

HELENA: But I'm not permitted to translate!

BALLAS: Why doesn't Otto do the translating?

STROLL: I can translate only after getting an authorization from Alex!

BALLAS: Then Alex will have to start granting the authorizations!

SAVANT: I can't, when nobody has the documents from Nellie!

BALLAS: Do you hear that, Nellie? You'll have to start giving people the documents regardless!

HELENA: But I'm not permitted to translate!

BALLAS: Why doesn't Otto do the translating?

STROLL: I can translate only after getting an authorization from Alex!

BALLAS: Then Alex will have to start granting the authorizations!

SAVANT: I can't, when nobody has the documents from Nellie!

BALLAS: Do you hear that, Nellie? You'll have to start giving people the documents regardless!

HELENA: But I'm not permitted to translate!

BALLAS: I'd like to know who thought up this vicious circle.

STROLL

SAVANT } *(in chorus)*: You did, Mr. Ballas!

HELENA

BALLAS: Well, what of it! The situation was entirely different at that time. Then it had a profound significance! But we've progressed since then, and that's why I propose the following simplifications in the procedure of translating all Ptydepe texts. These

will come into effect at once. First: Helena is permitted to issue the personal registration documents
without knowing the contents of the memos.
Second: Alex is permitted to authorize all translations without the personal registration documents. Third: Otto is permitted to translate without an authorization from Alex. Is that quite clear?
The fact that we can afford these measures is one
more eloquent proof of the rightness of our way!
(Hands his letter to STROLL.*)* And now—translate this for me!
STROLL *(reads)*: A protest. We, the undersigned staff
of the Accounts Department, protest most empha-
tically against the transfer of our offices to the
cellar and we announce hereby that we can no longer
work under these deplorable conditions—
BALLAS *(interrupts)*: That's enough! You may carry
on with your work.
*(*BALLAS *leaves by B.D.* STROLL, SAVANT, *and*
HELENA *stand about for a moment or two in silence,
then the B.D. opens a crack,* PILLAR *appears
and beckons them to follow him. They all leave by
B.D. Pause. Then* GROSS *and* GEORGE *enter by
B.D.* GEORGE *is livid, frowns, and furiously kicks
the coat rack, then the desk, spits, kneels down and
climbs on all fours through the secret door into the
observation cubicle. After a moment he indignantly
throws out Gross' fire extinguisher.* GROSS *takes
it and walks toward B.D. Just then* MARIA *enters
by B.D., carrying a paper bag full of limes. When she
sees* GROSS *she halts in surprise.)*
MARIA: Do you realize what would happen to you if
anybody saw you here?
GROSS: I'm no longer the Staff Watcher.
MARIA: Oh?
GROSS: Mr. Ballas has made me his deputy again.
MARIA: Congratulations!
GROSS: Good gracious, what for? Frankly, I'd rather
have remained the Staff Watcher.

MARIA: I know. You'll have to cope with some pretty
    nasty bits of business now, I expect.
GROSS: Never mind. Well, Maria, have a good time
    here. And do come and see me in my office one
    day. *(Slowly starts toward B.D.)*
MARIA: Mr. Gross—
GROSS *(stops)*: Yes?
MARIA: Has anybody translated for you that—you know
    —the thing you wanted to have translated yesterday?
GROSS: The memorandum? No. And according to current
    regulations, nobody can. Well, it's probably
    better that way.
MARIA: Do you think it's a negative one?
GROSS: I've learned always to expect the worst.
MARIA: Was any irregularity found during the audit
    in your department?
GROSS: Not that I know of. I did take the rubber stamp
    home just then, but I took it for reasons of work
    and not, as some people seemed to suggest, for my
    children to play with. My little Martin might have
    played with it at most twice in all that time.
MARIA: If your conscience is clear, you've nothing to
    worry about. Your innocence will be proved, but
    you have to fight for it! I believe that if one doesn't give
    way, truth must always come out in the end.
GROSS *(walks to Maria, sadly smiles at her and strokes
    her cheek)*: What do you know about the world,
    dear child! Still, I wish you could always stay like
    this! You're right, one really ought always to stand
    firm. The trouble is, I've never been very firm, more
    of an intellectual, always hesitant, always full of
    doubts, too considerate, a dreamer rather than a
    man of action—and that's my bad luck.
    (Pause.)
GROSS: When I think back, I see that I muddled up
    many things in my life myself. I often gave in too
    soon, yielded to threats, and I trusted people too
    much.
    (Pause.)

GROSS: If I ever have any influence on the course of
       things again, I'll do everything differently. More real
       deeds and fewer clever words! I've never been suf-
       ficiently matter-of-fact, coolheaded, proud, severe
       and critical—especially with myself.
       (Pause.)
GROSS: It may be partly because I belong to an odd,
       lost generation. We've given ourselves out in small
       change, we invested the best years of our lives into
       things which turned out not to be worth it. We were
       so busy for so long talking about our great mission
       that we quite forgot to do anything great. In short,
       we were a mess!
       (Pause.)
GROSS: But I believe that now I can at least face all
       this frankly, without hysteria and without self-pity;
       that I'll manage to recover from all the upheavals;
       that I'm still able to forget the past and make a
       quite new and quite different beginning.
MARIA *(moved)*: Have you the memo with you?
GROSS: You mean—surely you wouldn't—
MARIA: I'm quite grown up, thank you, Mr. Gross. I
       know what I'm doing. Give it to me!
       *(GROSS takes out his memo, hands it to MARIA,
       who reads it with growing excitement.)*
MARIA *(reads)*: Dear Sir, the last audit in your department
       has shown that the allegation of a repeated appropria-
       tion of the bank endorsement stamp for improper
       use is in your case entirely unfounded. On the con-
       trary, we feel obliged to emphasize the very positive
       findings of the audit, which clearly prove that you
       have been conscientious and responsible in the
       directing of your organization and that you therefore
       merit full confidence. This is further confirmed by
       your stand as regards Ptydepe, which has been quite
       unequivocal from the beginning. Our view of the
       Ptydepe campaign has always been entirely negative,
       for we understand it to be a profoundly harmful
       attempt to place office communications on a confused,

unrealistic, anti-human basis. We suggest that you liquidate with the greatest possible resolution and speed any attempt to introduce Ptydepe into your organization, and that you severely punish all those who have been propagating Ptydepe for their own personal advantage and in disregard of the consequences. Wishing you all success in your future work, we remain, yours faithfully, signature illegible.

GROSS *(after a moment, seriously)*: Thank you, Maria. Now at last I have an opportunity to prove that I have more civil courage than I've shown so far. I promise you that this time I shall not give way to anything or anybody, even at the risk of my position! *(Grabs his fire extinguisher and starts energetically toward B.D.)*

MARIA *(shyly bursts out)*: I like you—

GROSS: First I must deserve your sympathy, dear child! *(Leaves by B.D.)*
(Pause.)

GEORGE *(off-stage)*: That was a stupid thing to do, Maria.

MARIA *(frightened)*: Oh God! Are you there?

GEORGE *(off-stage)*: I came back a moment ago. And I'm not sorry I did. I hope you realize why!

HELENA *(off-stage)*: Listen—what about those limes?

MARIA *(softly)*: I'm afraid I do.

SCENE 10

The Director's office. BALLAS *is sitting at his desk,*
vainly searching his pockets for cigarettes. HANA *is*
combing her hair. GROSS *enters energetically by B.D.,*
carrying his fire extinguisher.

GROSS: Mr. Ballas, your era is over! My memorandum
　　　has just been translated to me and its contents make
　　　it perfectly clear that I'm not only quite innocent
　　　as regards the rubber stamp, but above all that I'm
　　　the only legitimate director of this organization.
　　　Furthermore, I'm requested by this memorandum
　　　to make an end of Ptydepe with the greatest pos-
　　　sible resolution and speed—

BALLAS: Hana—

HANA: Yes, Mr. Ballas?

BALLAS: Isn't it time for you to get your chocolates?

HANA *(looks at her watch)*: Oh yes, it is!

BALLAS: Well then, run along! And while you're there
　　　get me some cigarettes. The usual.

　　　(HANA runs out by B.D.)

BALLAS: Sorry. What did you say?

GROSS: Furthermore, I'm requested by it to make an
　　　end of Ptydepe with the greatest speed and to
　　　punish severely all those who were engaged in its
　　　introduction for their own advantage. In other
　　　words, history has proved me right and I, on the
　　　basis of the authority which is rightfully mine—

　　　(PILLAR looks in at S.D.)

BALLAS: In a minute, Mr. P.!

　　　(PILLAR disappears, leaving the door ajar.)

71

BALLAS: What did you say?

GROSS: In other words, history has proved me right and I, on the basis of the authority which is rightfully mine, shall draw due consequences from what has occurred. The way in which you seized the entire organization and forced Ptydepe on it cries for vengeance. I'm a humanist and my concept—
(HANA re-enters by B.D., carrying box of chocolates and packet of cigarettes. Hands cigarettes to BALLAS, puts chocolates in shopping bag, sits down and resumes combing her hair.)

BALLAS: Thanks, Hana. *(Lights cigarette with gusto.)* What did you say?

GROSS: I'm a humanist and my concept of directing this organization derives from the idea that every single member of the staff is human and must become more and more human. This is why I cannot but fight anyone who tries to spit upon this idea. I place the struggle for the victory of reason and of moral values—
(PILLAR looks in at S.D.)

BALLAS: In a minute, Mr. P., in a minute!
(PILLAR disappears, leaving the door ajar.)

BALLAS: What did you say?

GROSS: I place the victory of reason and of moral values above a peace bought by their loss. And I will carry on to the bitter end a struggle against all the misdeeds you've committed here. I think that under these circumstances it is no longer possible for you to remain in our organization. Kindly move out of my desk!

BALLAS *(offering GROSS a cigarette)*: Have one!

GROSS: I said, kindly move out of my desk!

BALLAS: Do have one, they're superb.

GROSS: Move out of my desk!

BALLAS: Let's say after lunch. All right?

GROSS: I'm glad you aren't putting up any resistance. After lunch will be all right.

BALLAS: I don't see why I should put up any resistance.

72

GROSS: You mean you agree with me?

BALLAS: Of course.

GROSS *(astounded, puts fire extinguisher on the floor)* :
Good gracious! How so?

BALLAS: I've seen the light.

GROSS: Have you?

BALLAS: Absolutely. I've come to the conclusion that
Ptydepe is all nonsense. I believed in it, I fought for
its establishment, but it was all a mistake. Sub-
jectively I meant well, but objectively the effect
was negative and so now I must accept, whether I
like it or not, all the severe consequences of my
activity.
(PILLAR looks in at S.D.)

BALLAS: One more minute, Mr. P.!
(PILLAR disappears, leaving the door ajar.)

GROSS: Are you being sincere? You ought not to be
so calm about it. It's very confusing.

BALLAS: I'm calm, because your severe but just words
express what I've been tragically feeling for a long
time, and so they fill me with relief that I won't be
obliged to continue any longer work which I don't
believe in, and that finally all my mistakes will be
put right. I wish you all the luck in your liquidation
of the disastrous consequences of Ptydepe, and I firmly trust that your work will succeed at least as much
as mine has failed. I'll help you to the limits of my
humble abilities. *(Offers GROSS a cigarette.)* Do have one!

GROSS: No thanks. You seem to have come to your senses.

BALLAS: I have.

GROSS: Perhaps you were indeed sincerely mistaken—

BALLAS: I was.

GROSS: How do you mean you'll help me?

BALLAS: Are you quite sure you won't have one?

GROSS: Thanks. Not now. How do you mean you'll
help me?

BALLAS: But they're really superb!

GROSS: I'm sure they are. How do you mean you'll
help me?

BALLAS: Look, old boy, if you don't take one, I'll be hurt! Well, as your deputy, of course.

GROSS: You must have misunderstood me. I said you'll leave the organization.

BALLAS: You wouldn't want to take such drastic measures, would you?

GROSS: I'm sorry, but I've made up my mind not to give way this time. I don't propose to repeat my old mistakes.

BALLAS: Come, come! Didn't I let you stay on as my deputy?

GROSS: That was different. Rightfully I should have remained the director, and truth was on my side.

BALLAS: I know that too, now!

GROSS: I've known it from the beginning.

BALLAS: It's always easy to be against a thing from the beginning! What is much harder is to be for a thing, even at the risk of getting your teeth kicked in!

GROSS: That doesn't change by one iota the fact that you are the chief culprit and so you must get the severest punishment. You'll simply have to pack up and get out!

BALLAS: And if I don't?

GROSS: You will!

BALLAS: Take it easy, old boy! *(Produces a sheet of paper and shows it to* GROSS.*)* Recognize this? It's the supplementary order for the introduction of Ptydepe and, if I'm not mistaken, it's signed by you, not by me. Or were you not the Managing Director at the time? Well then, who is the chief culprit?

(PILLAR looks in at S.D.)

BALLAS: Yes, Mr. P.—Give me another minute, will you?

(PILLAR disappears, leaving the door ajar.)

BALLAS: Well?

GROSS: That one signature is insignificant. It's nothing in comparison with what you've done.

BALLAS: Trouble is, history only knows such signatures.
GROSS: Besides, it was you who got me to sign it.
BALLAS: I did? I don't seem to remember.
GROSS: By your trick about the authentication of the notebook.
BALLAS: I wouldn't bring that up if I were you.
GROSS: Why not?
BALLAS: Because it's no extenuating circumstance at all. Just the reverse, in fact.
GROSS: I don't know what you're talking about.
BALLAS: Don't you? Well, look here, old boy. If it weren't for the notebook affair you might have claimed that you signed the order moved by a sincere belief in your principles, which, of course, wouldn't have excused your conduct, but would at least have explained it somewhat on humanitarian grounds; while if you do bring up this motive now, you'll be admitting thereby that you signed the order moved merely by petty cowardice? so as to avoid a piddling punishment for the notebook you didn't hesitate to plunge the whole organization into the jaws of the present catastrophe. Do you follow me? If, on the other hand, you hadn't signed the order, you might have pretended that you hadn't quite realized the impropriety of your action regarding the notebook, but your signature proves that you were clearly aware of this and that you panicked, because you were afraid of being punished. As you see, both your errors are intertwined in such an original way that the one greatly multiplies the other. If on top of your guilt in introducing Ptydepe you should now also volunteer an admission of your guilt regarding the notebook, you'd leave nobody in any doubt whatever about the real culprit responsible for all that's happened. Well then, shall we come to an agreement?
GROSS: All right, let's both resign.
BALLAS: As far as I'm concerned, I don't see why I should.

(Pause.)

GROSS *(faintly)*: And you would really honestly help
    me in everything?

BALLAS: I'm glad our discussion is at last reaching a
    realistic level. Of course I would. *(Offers him a
    cigarette.)* Take one.
    (GROSS takes it. BALLAS gives him a light.)

GROSS: You have a great deal of experience. You can
    work as stubbornly as a mule. Would you also work
    like a mule against Ptydepe?

BALLAS: I can't do things any other way.
    (PILLAR looks in at S.D.)

BALLAS: Yes, Mr. P. Nearly ready.
    (PILLAR disappears, leaving the door ajar.)

GROSS *(hesitantly)*: But somebody has to get the ax.
    You know how people are—

BALLAS: Leave that to me *(Calls toward S.D.:)* Ready, Mr.
    P.!
    *(PILLAR enters by S.D., followed by STROLL,
    SAVANT, and HELENA, all three carrying the folders
    they had in the last scene. They line up in a row and
    open the folders, as though about to sing in chorus.)*

BALLAS: You may begin.
    *(PILLAR gives them a hand signal and they all
    start solemnly reading.)*

STROLL, SAVANT, HELENA *(together)*: Dear Sir: The
    delegation which, under the leadership of Mr. Pillar,
    now comes to you consists of people who until the
    very last sincerely believed in Ptydepe and were in
    the vanguard of its introduction. All the more dif-
    ficult it is therefore for us, your loyal colleagues,
    to approach you now as a delegation whose mission
    it is to warn you against the consequences of any
    further propagation of Ptydepe. But precisely
    because we have done so much for Ptydepe we feel
    obliged to be the first to point out to you the insol-
    uble problems connected with its establishment.

BALLAS *(gestures them to stop)*: Dear friends. I know
    only too well, perhaps even better than you, how

desperate is the situation we've reached with Ptydepe, and I assure you that it has cost me many a sleepless night. As your former Managing Director I also accept the greatest share of the blame for the whole affair. We meant well, but we did wrong. In short, we sinned and now we must accept, courageously and without any feeling of being sinned against, the full consequences of our activities and with a redoubled energy struggle to remedy the damage we've done. In accordance with directives from the authorities I have taken certain first steps, with which I shall now acquaint you, because they are already specifically aimed toward a bold solution of the very problem which you have now come here to point out to me. First of all, I've resigned as your Managing Director and I've passed this position to the man who, as you'll surely agree, is the best qualified for it, Mr. Josef Gross. Mr. Gross who, throughout the era of Ptydepe, remained loyal to and even suffered for his convictions. I myself have received with gratitude from the hands of Mr. Gross the position of his deputy. I've received it in order above all to have an opportunity to show by diligent work my willingness to serve the new cause and thus to repair all the harm which, with the best intentions, I committed. And now let me give the platform to Mr. Gross.

GROSS *(embarrassed)*: What can I add? I'm not angry with you. I know that you meant well. The proof of it is also this your delegation, which comes in the name of reason and of moral values. Well, we should let bygones be bygones. Let us lose no more words over it. What is at stake now is the future. *(STROLL, SAVANT, and HELENA look questioningly at PILLAR. He gestures for them to turn the page. They begin to read further.)*

STROLL, SAVANT, HELENA *(together)*: We are sorry, but we cannot be satisfied with such a brief explanation. We threw our whole lives into the struggle for the wrong thing and we want to know who was responsible and who took advantage of it. We were deceived and we have the right to know who has deceived us.

GROSS *(softly to* BALLAS*)*: Will you answer this point?

BALLAS *(softly to* GROSS*)*: Yes. *(Louder.)* Friends! We are all guilty.

HELENA *(at Pillar's signal)*: That is only a hollow phrase!

STROLL *(at Pillar's signal)*: We want to know the actual persons!

SAVANT *(at Pillar's signal)*: The names.

BALLAS: All right then, I'll tell you. You've all surely noticed that for some time now there has been prowling about our offices a mysterious, silent man whose real function in our organization has never been known to us. I myself have come to know this man very well, because I've been under his direct surveillance. Inexhaustible was the well of methods by which he has been forcing us to do things we disagreed with. He pried into every nook and cranny, was always present, always subtly disguised in the cloak of inconspicuousness and of silent participation. And it is no accident that this gray eminence of Ptydepe, so diligently trying never to be publicly compromised in any way, has penetrated today— when the cause he served with such sycophancy is quite lost—to the head of your delegation, abusing your honest trust and averting from himself all suspicion by assuming the mask of a critical attitude toward Ptydepe.

(PILLAR, growing more and more desperate, turns from STROLL to SAVANT, from SAVANT to HELENA, but they all turn away from him. Dead silence. PILLAR runs in panic across the room, but stops at B.D.)

PILLAR *(shouts)*: Death to all artificial languages! Long live natural human speech! Long live Man!

(PILLAR runs out by B.D. An embarrassed pause. Then somebody knocks on B.D. All turn toward the sound. Pause. More knocking. Quizzical looks.

More knocking.)
GROSS: Come in.
        (COLUMN enters by B.D.)
BALLAS: Welcome, Mr. C.! Come in! This is Mr.
        Column.
        *(COLUMN bows to them, then sits in Pillar's
        place. General relief.)*
GROSS: Now then, let me conclude. What is at stake
        is the future. I appeal to you to put all your best
        efforts into the struggle for the re-establishment of
        natural human language, of our beloved mother
        tongue—
BALLAS *(interrupts)*: Wait a minute, Jo! Our colleagues
        are surely tired by now. We can talk tomorrow about
        what happens next. Now, let me suggest that we all
        go and have lunch together. Who's in favor?
        *(STROLL, SAVANT, HELENA, COLUMN and
        HANA at once raise their hands.)*
STROLL: That's an idea!
SAVANT: Bravo!
HELENA: Hurrah!
BALLAS: Let's all meet in a quarter of an hour at the
        Translation Center!
        *(STROLL, SAVANT, and HELENA hurry out by
        B.D.)*
BALLAS: Well, that's that. Are you quite comfortable.
        Mr. C.?
        *(COLUMN nods, walks to the desk, begins to col-
        lect the papers lying on it and to shove them in
        his pockets. BALLAS crosses to fire extinguisher
        hanging on the wall and takes it down. Then BAL-
        LAS and COLUMN leave by S.D.)*
GROSS: Things do seem to be moving rather fast.
HANA: Mr. Gross—
GROSS: There was nothing else I could do. An open
        conflict would have meant that I'd be finished.
        This way, as the Managing Director, I can at least
        salvage this and that.
HANA: Mr. Gross—

GROSS: Anyway, who knows, maybe this—Ballas—will turn out to be quite a good man after all. If I use him in the right place—

HANA: Mr. Gross—

GROSS: What is it?

HANA: May I go and get my lunch?

GROSS: Run along.

(HANA hastily takes her knife and fork and hurries out B.D. GROSS halts in the center and sadly stares ahead. BALLAS and COLUMN enter by S.D., both carrying their knives and forks, and walk toward B.D.)

GROSS *(to himself)*: Why can't I be a little boy again? I'd do everything differently from the beginning.

BALLAS: You might begin differently, but you'd end up exactly the same—so relax!

(BALLAS and COLUMN leave by B.D. GROSS lingers dejectedly for a second longer, then takes his fire extinguisher, hangs it in its original place, takes his knife and fork from the drawer and slowly walks out B.D.)

SCENE 11

The Ptydepe classroom. All four CLERKS *are back in their chairs, including* THUMB. LEAR *is lecturing.*

LEAR: The basic mistake of Ptydepe was its uncritical overestimation of the significance of redundancy. Redundancy turned into a veritable campaign, it became the slogan of the day. But it was over-looked that side by side with a useful redundancy, which indeed lowered the danger of incorrect in-terpretations of texts, there existed also a useless redundancy, consisting merely in a mechanical prolongation of texts. In the pursuit of maximum redundancy some eager clerks inserted within Ptydepe words—already long enough, thank you—even further so-called empty texts, thus blindly in-creasing the percentage of redundancy, so that the length of inter-office communications grew out of all proportion and sense.
*(*BALLAS *and* COLUMN *enter by B.D., carrying their knives and forks, cross the room,* BALLAS *pats* LEAR *appreciatively on the shoulder, then both leave by S.D.)*

LEAR: Let me give you an example. I've heard of a case where a brief summons to military H.Q. filled thirty-six typed pages single spaced.
*(*THUMB *giggles.)*

LEAR: Another disastrous manifestation is to be seen in certain stylistic habits which came into being dur-ing the Ptydepe era. The straining after maximum dissimilarity between what preceded and what fol-

81

lowed within a given text, out of which the habit
grew, was limiting more and more the possibilities
for the further continuation of texts, until in some
instances either they could continue only in one
specific direction, so that the authors lost all influence over what they were trying to communicate,
or they couldn't be continued at all.
*(GROSS enters by B.D., carrying his knife and fork,
starts toward S.D., but when he hears LEAR, he
stops and listens.)*

LEAR: All these mistakes have served as a sound lesson
in the creation of the new synthetic language—Chorukor—
which no longer attempts to limit the unreliability of
a text by a strenuous pursuit of words as dissimilar
from each other as possible; on the contrary it achieves
this by a purposeful exploitation and organization of
their similarity: the more similar the words, the
closer their meaning; so that a possible error in the
text represents only a slight deviation from its sense.
(GROSS hurries out S.D.)

LEAR: This method has many advantages, among them
the fact that Chorukor is very easy to learn. Often
it is enough to know only one word from within
a certain radius of meaning in order to guess many
other words of that group. We can do that unaided
and without any further study.

THUMB *(raises his hand)*: Sir!

LEAR: Yes?

THUMB *(gets up)*: Would you please demonstrate this
to us with an example? *(Sits down.)*

LEAR: Certainly. Monday becomes in Chorukor "ilo-
pagar," Tuesday "ilopager," Wednesday "ilopagur,"
Thursday "ilopagir," Friday "ilopageur," Saturday
"ilopagoor." Now, what do you think Sunday is?
Well?
(Only THUMB raises his hand.)

LEAR: Well, Mr. Thumb.

THUMB *(gets up)*: Ilopagor. *(Sits down.)*

LEAR: Correct, Mr. Thumb. You get an A. It is easy, isn't it?

82

(THUMB nods.)

LEAR: There you are! And at the same time the danger of an error can be entirely disregarded. For example, if a typist makes a mistake and instead of "ilopageur" writes in the announcement of a meeting "ilopager," the subject of the meeting is not at all distorted thereby. The most that can happen is that the staff will meet on Tuesday, instead of on Friday, and the matter under consideration will thus even be expedited.

SCENE 12

The Secretariat of the Translation Center. MARIA is standing dejectedly by her desk. BALLAS and COLUMN are there, both with their knives and forks. Noise of a party off-stage can be heard, as in Scene 6. MARIA begins to sob. BALLAS looks at her.

BALLAS: I'm sorry. I've promised Mr. Gross that I shall work like a mule and I don't want to break my promise by compromising on the very first day. What's going on next door?

MARIA *(sobbing)*: It's Mr. Wassermann's birthday, so his colleagues are giving him a party.

BALLAS: Paul Wassermann? Do you hear that, Mr. C.? It's Paul's birthday.
(BALLAS and COLUMN start toward S.D. Just then GROSS runs in by B.D., holding knife and fork in his hand.)

GROSS *(excitedly)*: Mr. Ballas!

BALLAS: Yes?

GROSS: What on earth does it mean?

BALLAS: What?

GROSS: Another artificial language is being taught here!

BALLAS: Chorukor.

GROSS: But we agreed, didn't we, that office communications are again to be conducted in our mother tongue!

BALLAS: I don't recall we agreed on anything of the sort.

GROSS: But my memorandum states quite clearly—

BALLAS: As far as I remember, it states nothing about

84

what language is now to be used here. Making an
end of Ptydepe doesn't mean that we must automatically give up all attempts at finally introducing
some precision and order into office communications.
If we did, we would—so to speak—throw out the baby
with the bath. Am I not right, Mr. C.?
(COLUMN nods.)

GROSS: But I understood that—

BALLAS: You understood wrong. It is evident that
you've lived for a long time in an isolation which
tragically marked you through the loss of a living
contact with reality. I don't want to meddle in the
business of the Managing Director, but when I see
that you're clearly fumbling and could easily come
into conflict with the opinion of most of our staff,
then I'm sorry but I have to interfere.

GROSS: Look, wouldn't it make things easier if you
carried on as the Managing Director and I as your
deputy?

BALLAS: Not on your life! I've already been foolish
enough to try that once already and I don't propose to do it again! Let's each do what suits him
best. I have certain organizational talents which J
can put to excellent use as your deputy, while you
can better bear the weight of responsibility connected
with the position of the Managing Director. *(To*
COLUMN:*)* They're still at it over there! Let's
go!
*(BALLAS and COLUMN leave by S.D. The noise of
the party grows louder, then quiets down.)*

MARIA: Josef—

GROSS: Yes?

MARIA: You didn't tell me the Watcher had come back.

GROSS: Well?

MARIA: He saw and heard everything!

GROSS: Everything? What?

MARIA: That I translated your memo.

GROSS: Well?

MARIA: He told on me and I was fired on the spot, be-

85

cause I'd translated an important Ptydepe text before passing my exams.

GROSS: But the use of Ptydepe has been cancelled—

MARIA: Mr. Ballas said that's beside the point. A rule
is a rule, he said. What guarantee is there, he said,
that I wouldn't someday make an improper translation from Chorukor as well. He said he had promised you to work like a mule and he didn't want to
break his promise the very first day by compromising.

GROSS: What are you going to do?

MARIA: Well, I hate to bother you, but couldn't you
perhaps reverse his decision? Or perhaps at least
put in a kind word for me?

GROSS: Dear Maria! We're living in a strange, complex
epoch. As Hamlet says, our "time is out of joint."
Just think, we're reaching for the moon and yet it's
increasingly hard for us to reach ourselves; we're
able to split the atom, but unable to prevent the
splitting of our personality; we build superb communications between the continents, and yet com-
munication between Man and Man is increasingly
difficult.

(Short pause. Noise of the party.)

GROSS: In other words, our life has lost a sort of higher
axis, and we are irresistibly falling apart, more and
more profoundly alienated from the world, from
others, from ourselves. Like Sisyphus, we roll the
boulder of our life up the hill of its illusory meaning,
only for it to roll down again into the valley of its
own absurdity. Never before has Man lived projected
so near to the very brink of the insoluble conflict
between the subjective will of his moral self and the
objective possibility of its ethical realization. Manipu-
lated, automatized, made into a fetish, Man loses the
experience of his own totality; horrified, he stares as
a stranger at himself, unable not to be what he is not,
nor to be what he is.

(Again a short pause. Noise of the party.)

GROSS *(turns directly to MARIA and continues with*

86

urgency): Dear Maria! You can't begin to guess
how happy I would be if I could do for you what you
just asked me to do. The more am I frightened therefore
that in reality I can do next to nothing for you, because I am in fact totally alienated from myself:
the desire to help you fatefully encounters within me
the responsibility thrust upon me—who am attempting
to salvage the last remains of Man's humanity—by the
permanent menace to our organization from the side
of Mr. Ballas and his men; a responsibility so binding
that I absolutely may not risk the loss of the position on
which it is based by any open conflict with Mr. Ballas
and his men.
(Pause. The noise off-stage culminates in unintel-
ligible singing which changes into cheers.)
VOICES *(off-stage)*: Hip, hip, hurrah!
(Cheers culminate in laughter which, however, soon
dies down. The party is over. While GROSS continues
speaking, STROLL, SAVANT, HELENA, HANA,
BALLAS, COLUMN, LEAR, THUMB, and three
CLERKS enter by S.D. GEORGE scrambles out of the
secret door. All have their knives and forks. All
stand in the background, waiting for GROSS to
join them to go to lunch.)
GROSS: Besides, there is no point in further compli-
cating my already complicated situation by taking
too tragic a view of your prospects. Let's try to be
quite matter-of-fact about it, shall we? You're still
young, you have a whole life ahead of you, you have
lost nothing so far. Just think! How many people
today are able to say with any degree of honesty
they have a brother with a theater group? A minuscule
minority! For all we can tell, one day you might come
to be thankful to Mr. Ballas for a career as a famous
actress. What matters now is that you must not lose
your hope, your love of life and your trust in people!
Chin up, my girl! Keep smiling! I know it is absurd,
dear Maria, but I must go and have lunch. So—good-
by! Be good! *(Joins others in the background.)*

They all look at MARIA.*)*

*   ): Nobody ever talked to me so nicely*

*   all slowly leave in a solemn, funeral-like proces-
    n by B.D., clutching their knives and forks.* MARIA
*takes her bag, collects her things, puts on her new hat,
looks about for the last time and then—happy—she also
leaves.)*